A Place in the Tent

Intermarriage and Conservative Judaism

Enlarge the site of your tent,
Extend the size of your dwelling,
Spare not!
Lengthen the ropes, and drive the pegs firm . . .
ISAIAH 54:2

A Place in the Tent

Intermarriage and Conservative Judaism

The *Tiferet* Project
Rabbi Mark Bloom
Rabbi Ted Feldman
Rabbi Gordon Freeman
Rabbi Stuart Kelman
Rose Levinson
Rabbi Harry Manhoff
Glenn Massarano
Rabbi Mimi Weisel

EKS Publishing Co., Oakland, California

Book Design
Irene Imfeld

Project Editor
Jessica W. Goldstein

EKS Publishing Co.
P.O. Box 9750, Berkeley, CA 94709-0750
email: orders@ekspublishing.com
Phone (510) 251-9100 • Fax (510) 251-9102
www.ekspublishing.com

First Printing July 2004

ISBN 0-939144-46-8

Contents

Preface

This work addresses the challenge of intermarriage as it affects Conservative Jewish life in America. Demographers currently estimate that nearly forty percent of American Jews marry non-Jews.[1] The following pages are intended to encourage and guide rabbinic, professional, and volunteer leaders in rethinking Conservative Judaism's response to intermarried households within the synagogue community.

Today Jewish experiences, obligations, and commitments guide many intermarried households, and non-Jews often join Jewish communities alongside their partners. They support their children's religious education, volunteer time on behalf of the congregation, worship on Shabbat and holiday services, and participate in Jewish home rituals. Our aim is to find ways to acknowledge this involvement and to support intermarried households within the framework of Jewish communal life.

Another goal is to increase the likelihood that the intermarried Jew will remain a strong and committed participant in Jewish life and institutions. We believe that finding legitimate ways of including intermarried households in Jewish practices allows us to nourish and sustain Jewish souls. Finding ways to say, "Come in. You are welcome in this synagogue—you and those closest to you" will bring Jews into the fold. Feeling integrated and welcome, rather than marginalized, usually affects the intermarried Jew more than his or her non-Jewish partner.

It is also our hope that intermarried households themselves will find this guide useful. Along with making the case for rethinking core Jewish concepts and approaches, we tried to clarify the issues and constraints the Jewish community grapples with when formulating its response to intermarriage.

This document is the work of the *Tiferet* Project, a consortium of Conservative rabbis who spent two years studying the issues of intermarriage. Four of the rabbis taking part in the *Tiferet* Project are the spiritual leaders of Conservative synagogues in Northern California. They are: Rabbi Mark Bloom, Temple Beth Abraham, Oakland; Rabbi Gordon Freeman, Congregation B'nai Shalom, Walnut Creek; Rabbi Stuart Kelman, Congregation Netivot Shalom, Berkeley; Rabbi Harry Manhoff, Temple Beth Sholom, San Leandro. The *Tiferet* effort also includes Rabbi Ted Feldman, executive director of Jewish Family and Children's Services of the East Bay, and Rabbi Mimi Weisel, former assistant dean of the Ziegler School of Rabbinic Studies at the University of Judaism. They were joined by Glenn Massarano, lay leader, and Rose Levinson, project director.

The *Tiferet* Profect's efforts focused on three areas:

1. Current policies within each rabbi's institutions and the rabbis' *halachic* and practical outlooks on intermarriage
2. Experiences of intermarried households
3. Historical, theological, textual, and programmatic ramifications of policy changes regarding intermarriage.

Please note the following about language usage: Within the Jewish community, there are several terms used to describe the committed relationship between a Jew and a non-Jew. We decided to apply the commonly used term "intermarried" because it most closely defines the population with which we are concerned. The term "interfaith marriage" will not be used because intermarried non-Jews often do not profess an active faith and/or they lack any formal religious affiliation. Furthermore, we urge the use of the term "household" rather than "family." In contemporary life, families and households are formed in ways undreamt of when the immediate family unit was the dominant modality for domestic life. "Household" covers the broadest range of situations.

The many communities constituting twenty-first-century American Conservative Judaism are not the same. Profound differences arise from the geographic distribution and sociological diversity of synagogues in the United States. In fact, the strength of the Conservative Movement lies in its ability to simultaneously celebrate and navigate the diversity that is a hallmark of contemporary Conservative Judaism.

We offer this document as one of many possible approaches to intermarriage. We have tried to articulate a coherent set of principles and concepts that add to and illuminate the conversation Conservative Jews are having today about this important issue.

We reached a broad consensus on key recommendations. In making the case for institutional change, *Tiferet* participants relied on the time-honored Jewish approach to complex issues—adherence to and argument with text.

We are grateful to the Walter and Elise Haas Foundation of San Francisco for their financial support, which made our discussions and this work possible. We also acknowledge the support of the boards and leadership of the participating institutions.

Acknowledgement and gratitude are more than due to the energetic, passionate, and professional support of Rose Levinson, who led us through this process.

1 ❖ Introduction and Basic Premises

The name *Tiferet* (beauty) derives from the *sephira* (aspect of the divine) in the symbolism of the *kabbalah* (mystical tradition). It unites the opposing forces of *gevurah* (strength) and *chesed* (kindness). In *kabbalistic* thought, *Tiferet* is a mediating force. We have attempted to address the issue of intermarriage from this conciliatory perspective, in which we weigh both our obligations to Jewish law and our need to reach out to marginalized members of the Jewish community. It is our hope that through this honest negotiation, our communities will find some measure of harmony and a renewed sense of *Tiferet*.

The title *A Place in the Tent* draws upon the biblical portrayal of the tent as a community's central meeting place. Particularly apt to our thinking is the following quote from Isaiah 54:2:

> *Enlarge the site of your tent,*
> *Extend the size of your dwelling,*
> *Spare not!*
> *Lengthen the ropes, and drive the pegs firm . . .*

As the authors of this document, we have spent many hours pondering the difficult questions of intermarriage. We worked to articulate guiding principles and studied traditional and contemporary sources. We also worked with intermarried couples. This book represents the accumulated wisdom and insight gleaned from this process. It is our hope that we have developed a context in which intermarried households can be welcomed into the synagogue community.

We affirm the sacred teachings of Judaism and its core values. However, we also recognize that these teachings and values often espouse an approach to Jewish life that excludes that which is "other." The Conservative Movement is challenged to confront the realities of family and household structure in twenty-first-century America. These realities include the presence of non-Jews who, by association with Jews, are deeply attached to the Jewish community.

The rabbis participating in this project affirm the following:

- Intermarriage is a reality in the life of many, if not all, Conservative synagogues. This reality needs to be acknowledged.
- Many Jews will be brought closer to Judaism if there is a recognized place for their non-Jewish partners in the community.
- There are many non-Jews who offer their spirit, time, and talents to the Jewish community.
- Without violating the spirit and/or letter of *halachah* (Jewish law) as interpreted in the Conservative Movement, there are ample opportunities for the creative integration of non-Jews into the life of the synagogue.
- Efforts to involve non-Jews in the community, including educational programs and a consideration of the non-Jew's role, will benefit Jewish family life and strengthen the community.
- Conservative synagogues need to find a way to acknowledge the presence of non-Jews and develop a meaningful process of integration.

Change is inherent in Judaism. The challenge facing the Conservative Movement has existed since its inception in the nineteenth century, namely, maintaining the integrity of *halachah* while simultaneously applying it to and interpreting it for new realities. The spirit of that tension permeated all of our discussions and the conclusions we reached in this undertaking. We paid serious attention to the arguments of those who believe that our recommendations threaten Judaism's core emphasis on endogamy. We have not abandoned that core principle. The rabbis who participated in this project want to strengthen the underpinnings of Jewish life by encouraging Jewish living and Jewish values in settings previously viewed as off-limits. We hope our work adds new dimensions to the life of the Conservative synagogue by welcoming all who would find therein a holy place and a community that values people for the deeds they perform.

Bruchim Habaim . . . welcome to those non-Jews who dwell among us and who share and shape our story.

2 ❖ Conceptual Underpinnings

*A single person (was created) to teach you that if anyone
who destroys a single soul of the children of Adam, the
Torah considers it as if he destroyed an entire world. Any-
one who sustains a living soul of the children of Adam, the
Torah considers it as if he or she sustains an entire world.
For the sake of peace among creation, that no person can
say to another, "(My) father is greater than yours" . . .*
(Mishnah c 4:5)

Over the centuries, Jews have expressed a variety of attitudes toward non-Jews. Living under hostile circumstances, Jews' attitudes towards non-Jews were negative. Loyalty was paramount in threatening environments. People who had business dealings with non-Jews were considered suspect, and those who married non-Jews were cast out of their communities and families. Obviously, this attitude prevented a non-Jew from participating in any aspect of Jewish life.

This unyielding attitude began to change when Jews found themselves living and working beside people of other faiths. Such proximity fostered a growing realization that people need to be respected as individuals regardless of their religious beliefs. At the same time, concern about the survival of the Jewish people continued, and intermarriage was seen as a threat to the Jewish future.

After the eighteenth century, Jews continued to accept the Enlightenment idea that an individual's worth is based on merit and not religious affiliation or ancestry. Jewish attitudes to non-Jews began to shift from hostility to ambivalence and tolerance.

In contemporary life, tolerance has moved towards acceptance of the other, and the rate of intermarriage continues to increase. It is unlikely this reality will change. The question that needs to be asked is not "How do we reverse this reality?" but rather "How do we address intermarriage in order to maintain Jewish continuity?" Many intermarried non-Jews are actively engaged in our communities. Those who are neither ready nor willing to convert to Judaism nevertheless support Jewish life and institutions. Without their efforts, many families would be lost to the Jewish people. We appreciate their often-enthusiastic willingness to be engaged in Jewish life in our homes and in our community, but we do not know how to express our gratitude within the bounds of Jewish tradition. We accept and embrace them as individuals, but we do not know how to acknowledge them in our liturgy and rituals, a situation that is particularly painful when our families experience rites of passage such as births, deaths, marriages, and *b'nai mitzvah*.

Theological Framework

Our responses rest on several interlocking principles. First is the universal principle, expressed in the Creation story, that every individual is intrinsically sacred and was created in the divine image—*b'tzelem Elohim* (in the image of God). The revolutionary teaching of Genesis is that we must treat people as individuals. In relating to others, we acknowledge that each person contains a divine spark. Therefore, negative attitudes towards non-Jews are not acceptable according to the theology of Genesis. It is not enough to tolerate a non-Jew, either. We must embrace each person and recognize his or her intrinsic worth as one who contains the divine spark. Everyone, Jew and non-Jew alike, is obligated to the covenant of Noah.[2] Thus, everyone has the opportunity to be engaged in a relationship with God. God is *melech ha'olam* (ruler of the world) not merely the ruler of the Jewish people.

Another principle derives from the covenant at Sinai, which articulates the boundaries that define membership in the Jewish people. While welcoming non-Jews who are intimately affiliated with our community, we acknowledge that our tradition includes certain obligations that are binding only on Jews. At the time of the Exodus, God established a covenant with an entire people, the descendants of Abraham. According to Jewish law, only those who are born Jewish or who convert to Judaism participate in this covenant, which sets out specific obligations to Jews. Thus, Jews are linked together as a community because we are bound by the same obligations; non-Jews, who are not bound by the Sinai covenant, do not share these obligations.

Jews can follow the Abrahamic covenant without negating the value or existence of others. Everyone is a member of the Noahide covenant that precedes the Abrahamic one, and thus each person has the opportunity to engage in a relationship with God. We do not claim to control God's actions or to know the divine will. Nor do Jews have an exclusive corner on redemption. Redemption comes to anyone who lives according to the principles of righteousness, justice and compassion.

Inclusion Versus Imposition

Because of our history, we must remember what it is like to have others attempt to impose their obligations on us. Throughout the centuries, people of other faiths have attempted to force Jews to abandon Judaism and to accept other religions. Usually, these people want to save Jews from damnation.

Jews, however, have no need to impose Judaism on others because Jews do not believe that redemption requires adherence to a specific theology. Being mindful of our own history, Jews must be careful not to impose obligations on people who do not have them by birth or conversion. We believe that each person in the extended Jewish community, Jew and non-Jew alike, can proclaim, "[T]he world was created for my sake" (Mishnah *Sanhedrin* 4:5). An inclusive community will value each person and still maintain the integrity of specific Jewish obligations.

In the Conservative community, Jewish obligations are defined by *halachah* and by norms. These laws and norms define what it means to be part of a Jewish community and what the obligations of membership are. Jews can fulfill their obligations without any negative attitude toward people who are not required to do the same, and the Jewish community can welcome and embrace non-Jews in its midst without imposing our obligations on them.

3 ❖ Values and Guidelines

While articulating roles for the participating non-Jew, we were guided by a number of underlying assumptions. First, our primary intent is to strengthen connections with the Jewish partner, who often feels marginalized. We recognize participating non-Jews as members of the Jewish community by virtue of their association with us. By making a genuine place for them, we make a place for the Jews who share their lives.

Definitions of "sacredness" (when based on perception rather than on *halachah*) need to be re-examined. Non-Jews do not impart *tumah* (ritual unfitness) to a synagogue, spaces or objects (e.g., the *bimah*/pulpit), the Torah or a cemetery. Therefore, it is often necessary to explain to congregants that permitting non-Jews to participate in certain ritual activities at the synagogue does not violate *halachah*. In these instances, the discomfort of some of the Jews in the synagogue must be addressed.

We recommend that the notion of *ma'arit ayin* (how things appear) be applied with extreme care, i.e., that it not be used as a default reason to forbid inclusion. Too often, the instinct to forbid something because of how it might appear eclipses the more positive need to do something for such reasons as *shalom bayit* (peace in the house) or *lifnim mishurat hadin* (going beyond the letter of the law.)

Moreover, we recognize the principle of *lechatchila* and *bediavad* (before and after the fact) as a major factor in *halachic* decisions. While we do not endorse intermarriage, we do argue that existing relationships should be honored and valued. Children of intermarriage should be encouraged and supported in their Jewish education. We recognize and reaffirm the Conservative Movement's commitment to matrilineal descent. Any child of a non-Jewish mother must undergo conversion before becoming a bar/bat mitzvah.

Because non-Jews do not have *halachic* standing, only Jews can fulfill a required *mitzvah* (commandment). Therefore, increasing the ritual role of the non-Jew does not diminish or change the *halachic* obligation of Jews. In fact, such concepts as *shalom bayit, kibud av v'em* (honoring one's father or mother) and *mipnei darkei shalom* (the ways of peace) are core values in Conservative Judaism that take precedence over consideration of the non-*halachic* status of non-Jews. In other words, honoring such concepts as peace in the house and respect for one's parents is more important than restricting the participation of non-Jews in certain activities.

When thinking about how to treat non-Jews, we urge consideration of the core values of Conservative Judaism. Letting those values predominate allows for new possibilities for welcoming intermarried households and thereby strengthening the community of Israel.

4 ❖ Framing a Response

The following sections, "Naming the Participating Non-Jew: *K'rov Yisrael*" and "*Halachic* Considerations," are the collective responses of the *Tiferet* rabbis, a consortium committed to finding ways of making a place for intermarried households within the Conservative Jewish *kahal* (community).

Our responses are bounded by *halachic* limitations, as well as by sensitivity to the hesitancies of community members who fear that such actions will weaken the institutions of Jewish life and discourage endogamy. While recognizing each rabbi's position as *mara d'atra* (teacher of this place) the final arbiter of all Jewish laws within a particular synagogue), we recommend that:

◆ The participating non-Jew be given a name, *k'rov Yisrael*
◆ The *k'rov Yisrael* be involved in select ritual activities
◆ The *k'rov Yisrael* participate in and be acknowledged during lifecycle events
◆ The *k'rov Yisrael* participate in non-liturgical synagogue activities
◆ The *k'rov Yisrael* have options for synagogue membership

K'rov Yisrael: Naming the Participating Non-Jew

Changes in demographics call for changes in Jewish vocabulary. Current realities dictate the need for a name for participating non-Jews, and naming non-Jews will strengthen efforts to bring Jews into the community by recognizing their non-Jewish partners.

We recommend that the term *k'rov Yisrael* (relative or friend of Israel, close to the Jews) be used as a designation for the non-Jew who is (or, as in the event of death or divorce, has been) partnered to a Jew and participates in and supports the Conservative synagogue community.

The term *k'rov Yisrael* is meant to be used internally within individual synagogues. The term is meant to apply to any non-Jews who are intermarried (or variously partnered) and affiliated with Conservative synagogues. It also applies to non-Jewish people who are widowed or divorced and seek to remain part of the community to which they belonged while partnered.

The Need for a Name

Non-Jewish persons have been inextricably linked with the history of the Jewish people and are an intimate part of our lives now. Naming them allows all of us to honor our interwoven commitments and obligations.

An analogy with the notion of *amicus curiae* (Latin for "friend of the court") is helpful. In legal terms, an *amicus curiae* is someone who is not a party to a lawsuit but who petitions the court or is requested by the court to file a brief on the basis of having a strong interest in the subject matter at hand. A *k'rov Yisrael*, like an *amicus curiae*, has no legal (*halachic*) standing. But he or she does have a strong interest in the matter at hand—in this case, Jewish law and custom as it pertains to being intermarried.

The name provides rabbis, lay leaders and Jewish educators with a handle as they work with intermarried families. Naming *k'rovei Yisrael* (plural of *k'rov Yisrael*) facilitates intermarried families making Jewish choices for their children, observing Jewish life fully in their homes and synagogues, and identifying with the ongoing story of the Jewish people.

Defining and naming someone acknowledges their existence. Jews have always privileged language, the naming of living things being one of the first tasks God gave to Adam.[3] Without a name, the individual is rendered invisible within the larger social order. Failure to designate the participating non-Jew who is partnered with a Jew reinforces the fiction that intermarriage is merely an isolated incident rather than an enormous presence in the fabric of contemporary Judaism.

Most important, giving participating non-Jews a name helps bring Jews into the synagogue and keep them once they arrive. Negating the existence of non-Jews who are intimately partnered with Jews drives a wedge between these Jews and the community. Caught in a conflict between the ties of marriage or partnership and those of belonging to a synagogue, many Jews will abandon the latter in the interest of the former. We seek to nourish and sustain Jews. Acknowledging the status and reality of *k'rovei Yisrael* is one way of doing so.

In the course of our studies, the issue of naming participating non-Jews engendered extensive discussion. While one person in our group voiced strong opposition to naming non-Jews, the rest of us asserted that finding an appropriate name was crucial to the very core of our mission. While we could continue the common practice of calling these individuals "non-Jews," the majority of us prefer to use the more positive term *k'rov Yisrael.* Designating people as "non—" is exclusionary; it labels people according to what they are not. Our intent in using the term *k'rov Yisrael* is for our community to grant status to those who are supportive of Conservative Jewish life without imposing Jewish obligations on them. Giving a name to participating non-Jews is a means of recognizing these people and acknowledging the contributions they make to our community.

Non-Jews Who are not *K'rovei Yisrael*

We acknowledge that there are people who stand outside of the Jewish tent and should remain there. Some of these people may consider themselves part of the Jewish people, but they proceed from premises that are confused at best and heretical at worst.

In determining who shall be excluded from the tent, we suggest three primary categories:
1. Those who proselytize and seek to convert Jews to another religion
2. Those born Jewish who have accepted the fundamentals of another religion
3. Those who, in the context of an intermarriage, are teaching their children to observe a non-Jewish faith in addition to or in place of Judaism

Identifying a *K'rov Yisrael*

It is up to the *mara d'atra* to determine who is a *k'rov Yisrael* and who is not. We are conscious, for example, that in certain communities this identification presents challenges. But because the *mara d'atra* determines applicability, there is built-in control around usage.

Our first concern is to create a category under which both practice and policy can be integrated. Our initial inclinations were to redefine existing categories from rabbinic literature, applying these definitions to current needs. We also noted that the issue of naming has been raised before, though not institutionalized.[4] Anecdotal evidence suggests that some rabbis already use such terms as *ger toshav* (resident alien; a stranger who dwells among the Jewish people) or *yirei shamayim* (God/heaven fearer) informally as a way of describing individuals with whom they come into contact.

Choosing the Term *K'rov Yisrael*

In the end, we rejected the biblical term *ger toshav* and the rabbinic term *yirei shamayim*. *Ger toshav*, a name imposed by the rabbis, is too reminiscent of *ger* as either a convert or stranger. "Resident alien" is not a comfortable designation, even if an analogy to citizenship is invoked. *Ger toshav* identifies the Jewish partner as the citizen and the non-Jewish partner as the resident alien or dweller among the Jewish community. The term re-enforces the notion of "outsider."

The term *yirei shemayim* has an unclear history. *Yirei shemayim* are infrequently mentioned in rabbinic literature. There is archeological evidence from the third century synagogue of Aphrodisias of the existence of *yirei shemayim* and their participation in the community's leadership. But rights and privileges of *yirei shemayim* are not defined in the literature.[5]

We choose *k'rovei Yisrael* as the best designation for those non-Jews who dwell among the Jewish people as the spouses, partners and children of Jews. People studying for the purpose of conversion would also be considered *k'rovei Yisrael*.

Finally, though this document recommends *k'rov Yisrael* as the designation for a participating non-Jew, the important point is that a name be utilized. The desires and needs of individual synagogues may recommend a term other than *k'rov Yisrael*. Whatever the choice, it is one that must be made and put into practice.

K'rov Yisrael and Conversion

We believe that Judaism offers positive, enduring teachings and that naming participating non-Jews and making Judaism accessible and understandable to them will encourage many to become Jews. Welcoming non-Jews opens the door to the possibility of conversion.

But designating persons as *k'rov Yisrael* is not an attempt to convince them to convert. In most cases, *k'rovei Yisrael* have no immediate intention to convert to Judaism. Some *k'rovei Yisrael* practice no religion, while others practice another religion outside the context of the synagogue.

The important point is that *k'rovei Yisrael* need to be recognized as partners with the Jewish people, whether or not they convert. They have cast their lot in with the synagogue community by their presence and by their social, financial, and political support. They cannot be ignored or treated as if they do not matter. It weakens both individuals and communities when *k'rovei Yisrael* are treated as a threat.

Jews are obligated by both *halachah* and custom. *K'rovei Yisrael* need to understand what the parameters and boundaries are for their participation in the life of the synagogue. Not being Jewish forecloses certain possibilities. The majority of *k'rovei Yisrael* are respectful of boundaries, particularly those that are time honored and based on strong ideological roots. Those deemed *k'rovei Yisrael* usually do not seek to dishonor constraints.

Concerns about *K'rov Yisrael*

We are sensitive to the concerns that naming *k'rovei Yisrael* raise. Among these concerns is the fear that naming non-Jews may encourage more out-marriage and discourage endogamy. Some also worry that in creating a new, inclusive category, the potential convert may be discouraged from choosing to become fully vested as a Jew by means of conversion. For many, the overarching fear is that in acknowledging the reality of intermarriage, we might abandon some of the fundamentals that have appeared to hold Jewish communities together over the centuries. We maintain, however, that for the vast majority of identified Jews, especially those who are affiliated with a synagogue, being Jewish is often about community and relationships.

Certainly for Jews, the religious and spiritual dimension is very important. But being "in community" is most often the tie that binds Jews to Jewish life. Given the primacy of community, it is incumbent upon us to explore ways in which *k'rovei Yisrael* may be viewed as part of the community. When they are not, it undermines our relationship to their Jewish partners and weakens their affiliation.

We acknowledge the reality of underlying fears and we respect the issues they raise. But we return to our core assumption: Significant numbers of intermarried families would join or become active in our

Conservative synagogues if they felt welcomed there and did not perceive themselves as being marginalized or rejected.

Designating a name for participating non-Jews and articulating specific ways in which they can be acknowledged sends an important message of welcome to the large number of intermarried households who wish to be a part of the Jewish community.

Halachic Considerations for the Role of K'rovei Yisrael

"May *k'rovei Yisrael* take part in synagogue ritual?" This document argues that a blanket "no" is neither the sole nor the most desirable response to that question. We acknowledge that each individual rabbi, as *mara d'atra*, determines the role of *k'rovei Yisrael* in the *halachic* life of his or her synagogue community. This section of *halachic* responses demonstrates the range of approaches available for responding to issues in this complex arena.

The process of *shealot u'teshuvot* (responsa) is quite old in our tradition and remains in use today. We arrived at twenty-one questions for this document. First, a group of intermarried couples worked together with members of the ritual committee in one of the *Tiferet* synagogues and developed a list of questions that reflected common concerns and experiences. Later, their rabbi refined these questions and the *Tiferet* project members placed them in theoretical groupings.

While the questions arose within the context of one particular synagogue, they illustrate core issues of ritual in any Conservative synagogue. The *Tiferet* participants used these questions to frame the range of *halachic* responses in this chapter. We offer these responses as representative approaches to the issues raised.

We discussed four major categories of questions. These are:

1. Participation of the *k'rov Yisrael*. For example: May a *k'rov Yisrael* serve as an usher or deliver a *drash* (sermon)?
2. Participation of families and children. For example: How does an intermarried couple announce the birth of a child? May *halachically* non-Jewish children attend religious school?
3. Participation of the Jewish partner. For example: May an intermarried Jew be employed by a Conservative congregation?

4. Participation of the rabbi. For example: May a rabbi attend the funeral of a *k'rov Yisrael* or the wedding of an intermarried couple?

Selected *Halachic* Responses

Following are selected responses from the *Tiferet* Project rabbis to questions concerning the participation of *k'rovei Yisrael*. We present responses to the questions most likely to arise in congregations as they look for ways to acknowledge the *k'rovei Yisrael* in their midst.

As might be expected, our deliberations produced a plurality of opinions for each question. This range of responses reflects the diversity of thinking inherent in this process.

We reiterate that each rabbi, as *mara d'atra*, will ultimately make decisions regarding ritual issues for his or her own synagogue. For intermarried households, the attitude rabbis and congregations bring to these deliberations is as important as the answers they give. Rabbis and congregations need to be sincere and humble when they decide how to set boundaries and communicate these boundaries to intermarried households. The rabbi's tone and attitude directly affect how Jews feel about synagogue life and whether or not intermarried households affiliate.

For each question below, a ◆ represents the response of a different *Tiferet* participant.

Participation of the *K'rov Yisrael*

May a *k'rov Yisrael* (KY) hand out *siddurim* (prayer books) and *chumashim* (the biblical readings for Shabbat and holidays) or be a greeter? May a KY stand alongside a Jew handing out *siddurim*? May a KY serve as a High Holyday usher?

◆ A *k'rov Isarael* may hand out *siddurim*. This is not a *halachic* issue. *Siddurim* and *chumashim* do not have any inherent *halachic* status. While they are *sifrei kodesh* (holy books), there is no restriction on contact between the KY and these items. Some people may be concerned that the greeter functions as a representative of the community. They will bring this issue under the *halachic* principle of *ma'arit ayin* and argue that *k'rovei Yisrael* handing out *siddurim* will give a false impression. However, non-Jews have been part of Jewish communities from the time of the giving of the Torah.

- There is sympathy for the requirement that, while it is permissible for a KY to hand out *siddurim* and *chumashim* and be a greeter, a Jewish representative of the community should also be present. A High Holiday usher is to be treated as a greeter.

- A KY may be a greeter because hospitality is a universally recognized norm. The issue of *ma'arit ayin* is not applicable. On the other hand, the principle of *darchei shalom* (for the sake of peace) does operate in this situation.

- One might be tempted to ask "What is the issue here?" Since a non-Jew can choose to observe *mitzvot*, and since *hachnasat orchim* (welcoming guests) is a core value, there should be no question that it be permitted. However, it might appear that the person who is handing out *siddurim* and *chumashim*, and who is standing and welcoming people into the congregation, is a full representative of the congregation. Clearly, there is no issue of *tumah* with regard to the physical objects. Since KY are an identified part of the congregation and we are studying these issues as they relate to their participation, a KY should be permitted and even encouraged to act as a greeter or usher. From this it follows that a KY may certainly stand next to his or her Jewish partner as well.

May a KY open the Ark? May a KY stand by his/her Jewish partner who is opening the Ark?

- While handing out *chumashim* and *siddurim* are clearly non-*halachic* issues, the ark is a more complicated one. While contact with the ark is not *halachically* forbidden, the perception by congregants may be different. Because of the connection with Sinai, there may be a sense of the sacred associated with the ark. Hence, a KY may not directly open the ark, but may be permitted to stand near it.

- Though there doesn't seem to be a *halachic* restriction, there are certain areas where a *siyag* (fence) should be erected in order to prevent constant, difficult decision-making, hurt feelings, and bickering in the synagogue community. Anything having to do with the Torah is one of these major fences. Opening the ark (which begins the process of re-enacting events at Mount Sinai), reading from the Torah, and reciting any blessing that includes *asher bachar banu* (who has chosen us) should be performed only by Jews.

- A KY may not open the ark because this is an important and specific honor defined by local, communal practice. The customs of the synagogue take precedence in these instances. For the same reason, the KY cannot stand beside a Jew opening the ark.
- Opening and closing the ark in ancient days was one of the most important honors, as it preceded taking out the Torah and reading from it before the entire community. Today, opening the ark does not carry the same weight and is usually considered a lesser honor than, for example, having an *aliyah* (going up to the Torah). Still, the symbolic act of opening the ark must be reserved for those who have the obligation to read the Torah, a group that does not include the KY.

What committees and committee chair positions are open to a KY?

- The KY cannot be the sole chair, but may be a co-chair. Only a Jew may chair the ritual committee. A KY can be a member of any committee, including the ritual committee.
- Almost every committee would be open, with the possible exception of ritual, since non-Jews shouldn't advise Jews on *halachic* matters. Some may argue that a KY should not chair a committee because of *ma'arit ayin* and because such a person is highly visible as a role model. However, to choose one example, a non-Jew may be the best person to chair the house committee or the personnel committee by virtue of experience. Why put someone else as chair who knows far less about these matters? Still, there are countervailing arguments. Furthermore, this decision probably falls under the aegis of the board, not the rabbi.
- Committees not directly dealing with liturgy and ritual may accept KY members.
- This question hinges on the definition of "membership." Since the KY is often considered an associate member, he or she may join any committee. Voting, however, is another matter, particularly on the ritual committee. In this case, the KY would be permitted to be present and engage in discussion, but may not vote. The issue of committee chair is the same as membership; that is, a KY may chair any committee except the ritual committee and the youth and adult education committee.

- Presumably, a KY is on a committee to enhance practice, not to surreptitiously disrupt it. Therefore, a KY is qualified to chair all committees of the synagogue. Sensitivity to *ma'arit ayin* should be given in areas such as the ritual committee and those offices or committees that represent the synagogue in the larger community. Within the synagogue, where roles and responsibilities are clearly delineated and defined, *k'rovei Yisrael* should be permitted to actively participate in all aspects of congregational governance.

What volunteer activities are open to KY members of families? May a KY serve as a teacher's aide, work in the front office, visit the sick, bake *hamentashen* (Purim pastries) or deliver *mishloach manot* (Purim gift baskets)?

- All volunteer activities are open to the KY with the following condition: If the activity is a specific *mitzvah*, then additional considerations may apply. For example, *mishloach manot* is a *mitzvah*. Just as in the case of a *shaliach tzibbur* (the person who leads the congregation in prayer), the person acting as an agent of the community must have the same *chovah* (requirement) as any member of that community. Therefore, a KY cannot act as the sole representative of the congregation. However, the KY may accompany the Jew. Another possible approach is that the KY may deliver *mishloach manot* so long as there are Jews with him or her.
- A KY may do anything except be a teacher's aide because the role of the teacher in religious schools is not only to teach Judaism, but also to help create future Jews by being a role model.
- A KY can voluntarily choose to observe *mitzvot*. Therefore, visiting the sick, baking *hamentashen*, and delivering *mishloach manot* would be permitted, *mipnei darkei shalom*. Being a part of the *Chevra Kadisha* (holy burial society) would not be permitted because performing this ritual requires the recitation of specific prayers, and there is a very strong custom that only Jews may perform this *mitzvah*. Working in the office is not a *mitzvah* per se and must be permitted. Serving as a teacher's aide would not be permitted because teaching in the context of a congregation requires commitment to the principles of the Jewish tradition. Learning, however, is open to all.

May a KY read a section of the service in English, including for the *Yamim Noraim* (High Holidays)?

- Only certain liturgical pieces have *halachic* status when recited in the vernacular, for example the *Shemah*, the *Tefilah*, and *Birkat Hamazon* (central selected prayers). Most prayers must be recited in Hebrew for them to count as fulfilling a religious obligation. Therefore, a KY may read English liturgical pieces other than those that have *halachic* status.

- A Jew must recite any prayer in which the leader's recitation requires the congregation to *yotzeh* (respond) or any prayer including the words "*asher bachar banu*" ("that chose us") or "*asher kideshanu bemitzvotav*" ("that made us holy through commandments"). Other prayers are open to the KY.

- *K'rovei Yisrael* may read English during worship as long as the English is not a translation of an obligatory part of the service (obligatory as defined by the *mara d'atra*).

- Every Jew has the obligation of prayer as set by the *matbeah* (the fixed portion of each service for weekdays, festivals, Shabbat and High Holidays). Since the KY does not have this obligation, he or she cannot take on this *mitzvah*. However, a KY may recite those English readings that fall outside the boundaries of the *matbeah*.

May a KY deliver a *drash* (commentary)?

- The *drash* has no *halachic* status. Historically, many synagogues have welcomed non-Jewish scholars, politicians and community leaders to address the congregation from the *bimah*. In many cases, these addresses have not occurred in the context of a Shabbat, festival, or daily worship service, but on special occasions such as dedications, community Thanksgivings, or the like. A non-Jew with no commitment to the Jewish community in no way imparts ritual unfitness to the *bimah*. In fact, as in the situations mentioned above, a non-Jew may bring honor to the synagogue and the Jewish community. Therefore *k'rovei Yisrael* may also go up on the *bimah*, address the congregation, and thereby honor the synagogue and Jewish community. Whether this is called a *drash* or an address does not affect this argument.

- Although the easiest answer is "no" because we're dealing with Jewish sensitivities towards certain rituals, objects, or events, we should look for ways to allow the KY to speak. Perhaps the *drash* can be given after the service.
- Yes. Interpretation is open to all. Again, to respect the Torah *siyag*, the KY should deliver the *drash* when the Torah is put away or rolled up. A non-Jewish interpretation of sacred text can be enlightening. Unlike the reading or blessing of the Torah, the person interpreting the text does not need to be *chayav* (obligated).
- It is assumed that each person who gives a *drash* speaks from his or her particular background and experience. When this person is a member of the congregation, there are certain assumptions that are clear to the congregation. When giving a *drash*, the KY should identify the framework from which he or she is speaking or be appropriately introduced. Listening to the teachings of a KY is certainly permitted. We all have studied the work of non-Jewish Bible commentators and learned much from them.

May a KY in an intermarried family be buried in a Jewish cemetery?

- It is proper to support the poor . . . to visit the sick . . . to bury the dead of non-Jews, to utter lamentation over them in *maspidim* (funeral ritual), and to comfort their mourners, in order to promote relations of peace (*Yoreh Deah* 151.12; 335; 367). Drawing on this directive, Kaufman Kohler and Jacob Lauterback wrote the following Reform response in 1914:

  "Unlike the Catholics, our cemeteries are not as a whole consecrated ground, in the sense that those not of the Jewish faith are excluded from them. Only the spot where the body is interred becomes sacred thereby. If, then, a Jew owns a lot in a cemetery, his right to bury his wife there is—from the Jewish standpoint—indisputable, unless the congregation or association which sells the lot has made stipulations or conditions forbidding the burial of non-Jews in the cemetery. Of course, it is understood that a non-Jewish service or symbols of another faith are prohibited."

  The Conservative *Beit Din* (Rabbinic Court) in Oakland, California, concurs with this interpretation in its May 14, 1993

"Responsa on Jewish Cemeteries:" "In terms of the service, for the non-Jewish partner or child [or parent or sibling], no Hebrew or traditional prayers would be used and while Biblical selections may be, they should be done in English. Poetry and eulogies are obviously permitted."

- Yes, if the deceased was the partner of a Jew. However, there must be limits so that the graveside funeral is a non-sectarian service. The gravestone must not contain religious symbols.
- Possibly if there are no non-Jewish religious symbols there, but it may be that we have to segregate more in death than in life, to respect the wishes and intent of those already buried.
- A local *Beit Din* addressed burial a few years ago. Each *kever* (grave) is regarded as a separate entity. However, it is not permissible to bury someone who practiced another religion in a Jewish cemetery. There is also a question of *ma'arit ayin*, that is, what makes a cemetery Jewish is that Jewish people are buried there. The rabbi may participate in the burial of non-Jews by giving a eulogy, but he or she may not perform any Jewish liturgy.

May a KY be a member of a congregation?

- The United Synagogue says "no," and the *Tiferet* Project has spent considerable time discussing associate member status. When we tell people associated with our synagogues that they do not count as members, we run the risk of harming *shalom bayit*. Furthermore, in many instances, partners contribute towards the cost of membership without any of the benefits. Nevertheless, that is the current policy of virtually all Conservative congregations. United Synagogue should consider household memberships. At a minimum, all mail from the synagogue should be addressed to both partners in a household.
- A KY cannot be a member of a United Synagogue Conservative Jewish congregation. We might want to create an associate member status. In such a case, the KY would be asked not to engage in decisions regarding liturgy or ritual or to vote at congregational meetings.
- A Jew is defined in our Conservative congregation as someone either born of a Jewish mother or converted. A KY, according to our

by-laws, is considered an associate member. The by-laws regarding membership state:

"Jews are eligible for membership in this congregation. Non-Jewish spouses and dependents and non-Jewish children of members may become associate members....Associate members may attend religious services and participate in congregational activities except for voting at congregational meetings or serving on the Board of Directors. Participation of associate members in Jewish ritual shall be limited to roles permissible within *halachah*, as defined by the rabbi in consultation with the Ritual Committee."

◆ Membership in our synagogue is granted to a household, regardless of the number of Jews living in that household. Each membership has a single vote at congregational meetings.

A household, with or without children, is defined as:
a. married couple/gay couple, endogamous
b. married couple/gay couple, intermarried
c. single, divorced, or widowed Jew
d. non-Jewish widow/widower of former Jewish member
e. divorced, formerly intermarried non-Jewish member

Participation of Household Members and Children

Is it permissible to announce the birth of a child into an intermarried household at services?

◆ Yes. It is a joy for a member family, regardless of status. This is a simple way to be inclusive.

◆ To forbid the announcement of the birth of a child in an intermarried household is not only silly, but is also impractical.

May an intermarried household sponsor a *kiddush* celebrating the birth or adoption of a non-Jewish child?

◆ Making the distinction in many of these next questions between *lechatchila* (before the fact) and *bediavad* (after the fact) is central. If a birth or adoption has already occurred and the child is therefore now a member of the family, it is permissible to sponsor a *kiddush* so long as the child will be reared as a Jew.

- A family may not sponsor a *kiddush* celebrating a birth or adoption of a non-Jewish child unless there is a commitment to convert that child to Judaism.
- At issue here is the household unit and the concern for *shalom bayit*. Legal decisions were often made for the sake of the harmony of the household, implying that this core value takes precedence over others in certain instances. We believe this is one such instance and would permit the *kiddush*.
- Yes, assuming that the child is to be reared in a Jewish family.

May a KY accompany the procession or recession of the Torah during a child's bar/bat mitzvah?

- This is not a *halachic* issue, although accompanying the Torah may be perceived by congregants as happening within sacred Jewish space. However, because a a bar/bat mitzvah is an important celebration for a family and because the KY has helped prepare the young person for this day, the practice should be permitted.
- Yes. There is the worry about the Torah *siyag*, but it is simply too hurtful and awkward to exclude the KY from this sacred family moment. The KY does not carry the Torah, but simply accompanies the child as he or she does it. This position is an appropriate metaphor for the KY who helps rear a Jewish child.
- The KY may not accompany the Torah procession at the time of a child's bar/bat mitzvah because of *ma'arit ayin*.

May *halachically* non-Jewish children attend religious school? Should they be treated as full family members in the context of the synagogue?

- The answer is yes with a caveat. Children under the age of bar/bat mitzvah should be treated as members and should be allowed to attend religious school. Allowing full participation will encourage the child and his or her family to pursue Judaism. However, the situation becomes more complicated once the child has reached bar or bat mitzvah age. For example, if a young person is past bar or bat mitzvah age and is asked to lead services or *kiddush*, the *halachic* status of the child complicates the issue and could entail restrictions. We need to think about this situation and find creative solutions.

Ideally, we will find ways to include these young people. If they choose to be involved, they are demonstrating an interest in and commitment to Judaism.

- No. Full inclusion encourages families to postpone making a decision about how they will rear their child. In striving for clarity, we do not want to encourage ambiguity. To put off making this decision until the age of bar/bat mitzvah is the worst thing parents can do, as the family's stress level is much higher at that time. There are some exceptions, such as pending conversions.

- If the children are pre-bar/bat mitzvah age, they should be included in High Holiday tickets, invitations to synagogue events and participation in the religious school with the understanding that they cannot become a bar/bat mitzvah without conversion.

- Children up until the age of majority should be encouraged and supported in their Jewish education. In order to celebrate a bar/bat mitzvah, the new adult must formally convert.

May a KY stand at the *bimah* when a Jewish family member is honored with an *aliyah* to the Torah on one of the following occasions: a baby naming/adoption, an anniversary, the bar/bat mitzvah of a child, the Shabbat before a wedding or *brit reyut* (commitment ceremony)?

- *Krovei Yisrael* have no *halachic* status when standing on the *bimah*. There is no prescribed distance that *k'rovei Yisrael* must maintain in relation to the Torah. We find some guidance in the *Shulchan Arukh* (codification of law). In the event of a fire, the *Shulchan Arukh* rules that a gentile may carry a Torah out of the building. The *Shulchan Arukh* also rules about buying a Torah from a gentile. It is clear from these two cases that a gentile does not impart ritual unfitness to the Torah. Therefore, standing near the Torah does not impart ritual unfitness to the Torah either.

- *K'rovei Yisrael* should be allowed to stand on the *bimah*. However, only Jews can fulfill the community's obligation to recite a *brachah*, (blessing) so the *aliyah* itself must be given to a Jew. The presence of others on the *bimah* does not change this situation. *Krovei Yisrael* should be careful to recite only those prayers, blessings or readings that they can honestly say with a sincere heart.

◆ To say "who chose us" one must accept the covenantal responsibilities implied in that blessing. Furthermore, in praying one should understand the meaning of the prayers. This precept also has profound implications for Jewish participants in the worship service. It is not the rabbi's responsibility to police who is sincere and who is not sincere. The rabbi as teacher must instruct the congregation in the obligation to respect the prayers of those who are sincere, and to refrain from demeaning the value of prayer by simply reciting words or sounds.

◆ Non-Jews may not stand at the *bimah* during an *aliyah* because of *ma'arit ayin*. We do not want to give the impression that the non-Jew is fulfilling an obligation incumbent on a Jew.

◆ Any Jew may have an *aliyah*, but during an *aliyah* on the Shabbat preceding an intermarriage, no *misheberach* (prayer for divine support) for the wedding couple shall be said.

◆ In the case of an anniversary, since this is *bediavad* (after the fact), the Jewish partner could come to the *bimah*, have the *aliyah*, and then be joined by the non-Jewish partner for a *misheberach*—provided the KY is not practicing another religion. Similarly, in the case of a bar/bat mitzvah, the Jewish parent may come to the *bimah* and say the words for the *bracha* (blessing). Once completed, the KY parent may stand next to the Jewish partner while the appropriate *misheberach* is said, again provided the KY is not practicing another religion. These responses are based on the fact that the event (birth, wedding, or rearing of a Jewish child) has already occurred.

◆ Standing at the Torah during an *aliyah* may or may not technically be a *halachic* issue. Group *aliyot*, in general, are not done except in special circumstances. In any case, this involves what is considered sacred space. Variables must be weighed with a bias towards inclusion and recognition.

◆ To continue the metaphor of the Torah *siyag*, certain blessings involving intermarried households should be done off the *bimah*, or at least away from the Torah, but they should definitely be done.

In an intermarried household, who can be involved in a baby-naming *aliyah* in the synagogue, and what restrictions, if any, apply to either parent?

◆ Since this is *bediavad*, the Jewish partner could come to the *bimah* with the baby, have the *aliyah*, and then be joined by the non-Jewish partner for a naming and *misheberach*.

Under what conditions may a *misheberach* be said?

◆ For the sake of *mipnei darchei shalom*, a KY may be included in a healing *misheberach*.
◆ For a *misheberach* to be recited at a rite of passage (birth, wedding, bar/bat mitzvah, etc.) the general principle (to be decided case-by-case) is that if the event has already occurred, the *misheberach* is permitted.

May a *halachically* Jewish person be called for an *aliyah* using the name of both parents if one of those parents is a KY?

◆ The name of a non-Jewish parent must not be included when called for an *aliyah*.
◆ A Jewish name testifies to an individual's Jewish lineage. Converts, for example, are called the son or daughter of Abraham and Sarah. They inherit all of Jewish history. Because one's Jewish name contains a list of Jewish lineage, it cannot contain the name of a non-Jewish parent. Converts or patrilineal Jews may include their Jewish parent's name in their own.

Participation of the Jewish Partner

May a Jewish partner in an intermarriage be employed by the congregation?

◆ Absolutely—despite the *teshuva* by the Committee on Jewish Law and Standards to the contrary. Our congregation has questioned this issue in other written documents.[6]

Participation of the Rabbi

May the Rabbi attend a wedding reception of a Jew and a non-Jew?

- Invoking the principle of *bediavad*, it is permissible to attend the reception, but not the wedding itself.

May the Rabbi give a benediction at the wedding reception of a Jew and a non-Jew?

- While the rabbi may attend a wedding reception of a mixed marriage, he or she may not give a benediction or greeting.
- If it were certain that the couple planned to raise their children as Jews, then the rabbi might offer some words of congratulations. However, he or she may not use some of the more traditional forms of blessings.

May the Rabbi participate in the burial of a *k'rov Yisrael*?

- The rabbi may be present for the burial of a *k'rov Yisrael* in a Jewish cemetery if the *k'rov Yisrael* did not practice another religion. The rabbi may offer words of comfort or deliver a eulogy.

5 ❖ Challenges of the Rabbinic Role

The Rabbi's Role in Ritual and Law

We begin with the following assumptions about the role of the rabbi today:

- A Conservative rabbi's role regarding *halachah* is to determine how ritual is implemented within his or her synagogue.
- Some decisions are based mainly on interpretation of Jewish law, while others are determined largely by *minhag* (custom).
- Sociology, psychology, precedent and communal norms and beliefs are key factors influencing rabbinic decision-making.
- The rabbi of a given synagogue has the option of deciding who in his or her congregation is a *k'rov Yisrael* and in what rituals *k'rovei Yisrael* may participate.

Concerns of the Congregation: Halachah (Law) and Minhag (Custom)

Communities legitimize a rabbi's manifold roles explicitly (with a job description) and implicitly (according to a community's customs and norms). Many rabbinic functions result from a community's unspoken expectations and desires. For example, it is not *halachically* necessary for a rabbi to be present at a *brit milah* (ritual circumcision). However, most congregants expect their rabbi to be present at these kinds of lifecycle events. This expectation and its fulfillment reinforce the contract between rabbi and congregants and illustrate the intimate relationship a rabbi has with members of his or her synagogue.

This intimacy plays a part in all rabbinic functions. Interpreting *halachah* may seem to be a largely technical, legal function. In reality, however, deciding upon *halachah* is also an exercise in sociology and psychology that takes place within a particular synagogue community.

When making a ruling, the rabbi takes into account the values, customs and priorities of his or her synagogue.

The rabbi, as *mara d'atra*, functions neither in a realm of absolutes nor in a world free of ambiguity. No rabbi aims to make *halachic* pronouncements that the majority of his or her congregants are unlikely to follow. It is incumbent upon the rabbi to understand the congregation's prevailing culture and expectations and to factor these into decision making.

This mutuality between the rabbi and the congregation has a great deal to do with the perception of the rabbi as the main keeper of tradition. Much like the biblical *kohanim* (priests), today's rabbi often establishes and maintains boundaries to the holy. These boundaries are both physical (i.e., the *aron hakodesh*/ark) and spiritual (who takes part in what ritual, who recites which prayers). The rabbi decides who is permitted to cross the boundaries, and how one is to have access to sacred space and to be part of an activity in sanctified time (like Shabbat).

Concerns about the Perceived Sacred

Each rabbi must remain sensitive to the apprehension some Jews will experience at any notion of *k'rovei Yisrael* crossing into perceived sacred space. Helping congregants understand when and how this space is navigable is as great a part of the task at hand as educating *k'rovei Yisrael* on the limits of their participation.

To take one example, whether a *k'rov Yisrael* may be on the *bimah* during an *aliyah* is a decision made by the rabbi as *mara d'atra* for his or her synagogue. In making the decision, the rabbi must be sensitive to the fact that many Jews see an *aliyah* as a sacred act performed in a sacred Jewish space. Recognizing and acknowledging the weight Jews place on a particular act in a certain space is a delicate and complex matter

In maintaining sacredness, rabbis are aware that boundaries are often decided by factors having nothing to do with biblical precedent or rabbinic interpretation. Changes in liturgy, for example, have sometimes been a response to oppressive environments. For example, many argue that the limited access women have historically been given to certain aspects of Jewish life is a culturally imposed boundary, having its basis in a male dominated world view.

Another tension lies in determining whether or not an issue is *halachic*. Many issues may appear at first glance to involve Jewish law but will turn out to be questions best decided by the synagogue board or another committee. Determining what areas are within the purview of the *mara d'atra* and which are not is part of the synagogue's decision making process.

The approach rabbis and synagogues take in answering difficult questions will bear directly on how Jews feel about their synagogue and whether or not intermarried households choose to affiliate.

Impact on Role and Participation of K'rovei Israel

The multiplicity of roles included in the job description of today's congregational rabbi reflects the evolving nature of the modern rabbinate and its inherent struggles. All major rabbinic functions—rabbi as teacher and counselor, rabbi as keeper of tradition, rabbi as guardian of boundaries—have particular ramifications regarding intermarried households.

Intermarried households are an integral part of Conservative synagogues. *K'rovei Yisrael* make many contributions, including rearing Jewish children. Together with their Jewish partners, they deserve to be acknowledged, particularly at lifecycle events. And, most often, it is the Jewish partner for whom this is most important. When the congregational rabbi finds ways of acknowledging *k'rovei Yisrael*, it brings Jews into the synagogue.

A key challenge comes when rabbis try to find ways to allow *k'rovei Yisrael* to participate in Jewish ritual and custom, usually as part of a lifecycle event. Deciding how and when to include *k'rovei Yisrael* involves grappling with a number of variables, including the rabbi's own understanding of what is permissible, the meaning and weight assigned by congregants to specific acts and rituals, and the education of synagogue members as to which boundaries are permeable and which are not.

The Rabbi as Counselor

For many in the Jewish community, the rabbi's most important role is that of counselor, comforter and source of personal support. It is certainly important for most congregants to know that their rabbi can perform public rituals effectively. However, it is the personal, supportive relationship that the members of the community most often seek.

Grounded in *mitzvot* such as *nichum avaylim* (comforting the mourner) and *bikkur cholim* (visiting the sick), the rabbi is called upon to be a wise and comforting presence to congregants. Even if the rabbi eschews the role of direct counselor, he or she is expected to sympathize and empathize with the many struggles confronting individuals and families. The rabbi's ability to do so is seen as a prime qualification.

Sometimes a rabbi's role as counselor comes into direct conflict with the rabbi's role as *mara d'atra*, the latter of which demands setting boundaries and enforcing standards. This happens frequently at lifecycle events such as when young people become *b'nai mitzvah*. Often the rabbi is asked to accommodate any and all family members who wish to take part in the service. Sometimes such accommodations are difficult or impossible. What is to be done, for example, when the family of a bar/bat mitzvah ask that a family member involved in a messianic synagogue be given an *aliyah*?

The rabbi has to set boundaries within the context of Conservative Jewish standards, but such actions often intrude into the pastoral, personal relationship the rabbi has with a family. This tension cannot always be resolved. At times, it simply is a reality inherent in the situation.

The conflict between counselor and *mara d'atra* roles is particularly powerful when rabbis attempt to negotiate the line between welcoming the non-Jewish partner in a marriage and the Jewish preference/requirement for endogamy. As counselor, the rabbi is called upon to welcome and support the intermarried household who has chosen to affiliate with the synagogue. This can set up a contradiction between maintaining boundaries and appearing to accept intermarriage.

Within the Conservative Movement, a complete resolution is elusive if not impossible. No single approach will satisfy all rabbis and congregational leaders. But there are some positions that, when taken, may inform, enlighten, and strengthen the rabbi's role as counselor.

The first such position is a resolute willingness to deal with the changes in the demographics of the American Jewish community. As noted, demographers estimate that almost half of today's newly married Jews are partnered with non-Jews. A number of these intermarried couples want to affiliate with a Conservative synagogue. It is incumbent upon rabbis to seek ways to relate to and be engaged with intermarried households who are part of their synagogue community.

It is equally important to honor the commitment of intermarried Jews who, regardless of their partner's circumstances, remain part of the Jewish community. By extension, this action frequently involves the rabbi's relationship with the *k'rov Yisrael*.

6 ❖ Rethinking Synagogue Membership

In the past, ritual and observance was done outside synagogue walls. Much of it has now moved inside this institution. Many Jews today look to the synagogue as the primary place where they "practice" Judaism. This reality presents the modern Conservative synagogue with challenges, particularly as it considers how best to include intermarried households and partnerships in its membership and in its governance activities.

A synagogue is a Jewish institution based upon Jewish laws, traditions and customs. It exists to meet the needs of its members as individuals and the Jewish community as a whole. In modern times especially, the synagogue occupies a central role in helping people feel they live a Jewish life and are part of *klal Yisrael* (the community of Israel).

The recommendations for synagogue membership and governance that we make here and in the *Halachic* Responses section rest on some fundamental assumptions and observations. First, we assume that *k'rovei Yisrael* follow the six or seven Noahide laws, which entitles them to a place in the *Olam Haba* (world-to-come). We note that Judaism is one of the few world religions with room in its afterlife for the non-believer. Second, there is historical precedent for our suggestions. We know that in some ancient Jewish communities, *k'rovei Yisrael* were active participants and even officers of the community. Third, and perhaps most crucial, we have observed countless numbers of intermarried households in which *k'rovei Yisrael* help rear Jewish children, financially support Jewish institutions (including but not limited to the synagogue), and participate actively in performing fundamental tasks that ensure Jewish continuity.

Membership questions are controversial, as boundaries are most clearly enforced through denial of membership. We recognize that the membership issue is potentially very divisive, both within individual congregations and in the current debate in national Conservative Jewish circles. It is a crucial issue that elicits more than one response. We have previously presented a number of possibilities in the *Halachic* Responses section.

As suggested earlier, we recommend identifying the member unit as a household rather than a family or individual. We further recommend giving each household a single vote. Currently, many congregations give one vote to each Jewish member, thus invalidating the involvement of the non-Jewish partner. Granting one vote to each household provides one more way to reach out to the *k'rov Yisrael*, thus encouraging full involvement of both partners.

Moreover, allowing one vote per household eliminates a number of problems. In households with teenagers over twelve years old, it eliminates the need to count each of the young *b'nai mitzvah* as members with a vote. It minimizes the feeling of single people and widows/widowers that they count less than those with partners or spouses. And most important, it does not devalue the non-Jewish spouse.

Finally, we believe it is essential that the professional staff of the synagogue serve all households equally, regardless of the number of Jews living in it. We further stipulate that all people, whether Jew or non-Jew, be treated with equal respect.

Conclusion

For everything there is a season, a time for everything under heaven.
(Kohelet 3:1)

Now is the time for the Conservative Jewish community to examine honestly the challenge of making a viable place for the many intermarried households who wish to be part of the Jewish story. It is possible, but not sensible, to continue to ignore the impact of intermarriage and to make access to synagogue life difficult for *k'rovei Yisrael*. Doing so, however, will inhibit affiliation and participation of the Jewish partner.

Encouraging conversion is one response to intermarriage, and this document does not diminish that stance. However, Kohelet also reminds us that "there is nothing new under the sun" (1:9). Historically, large numbers of *k'rovei Yisrael* lived amongst Jews.[7] Judaism survived and flourished in those times, as it will now.

The question of how to ensure Jewish continuity elicits various responses. Ours is to articulate ways in which a genuine place can be made for intermarried households within the communal tent. We argue that by doing so, many Jews who feel there is no place for them or for their Jewish children will come to be a vital part of the Conservative synagogue community and, by extension, the larger Jewish community.

This document articulates concepts to help foster inclusion. One key recommendation is naming the participating non-Jew *k'rov Yisrael*. Included are suggestions regarding the participation of *k'rovei Yisrael* in lifecycle events and other synagogue rituals. We have also presented a historical and conceptual framework for viewing intermarriage and discussed some of the challenges inherent in the complex role of congregational rabbi. Finally, we have presented a range of *halachic* possibilities for rabbis to consider as they decide whether and how *k'rovei Yisrael* may participate in their synagogues and communities.

Fundamental to our thinking is the notion that we must find rituals to honor those moments in every person's life that are key markers in the journey from birth to death. The intermarried who dwell amongst us give us many gifts, including their Jewish children. It is our task to acknowledge that they are part of our shared destiny and to "enlarge the size of our tent" so that together we may live out an enriched Jewish story.

Appendix A
Rethinking the Jewish Narrative

Foundation Stories:
The Role of Narrative in Defining Community

Communities do not exist in a vacuum. Those who count themselves as members of the same community share a common story that provides unity and coherence. Various names are given to these underlying stories, including operative ideals,[8] value concepts,[9] and foundation myths.[10] These narratives form the basis for what is seen as essential to the community. Foundation stories set the course and destiny for those who count themselves as part of a group. They are a key factor in defining where and how boundaries are set, who is in and who is out, what is required and what is expected.

As times change, the stories are reinterpreted to make them applicable to new situations. Sometimes a foundation story loses relevance to a given community. When this happens, the narrative must be reshaped to fit new realities.

Reshaping foundation stories is no easy task, and it is one that happens gradually. Those who articulate the framing stories for the Jewish community find themselves grappling with texts,[11] with law and custom, and with the reality of life for a community at a particular time and place.[12]

Attempts to change the narrative always encounter resistance. A fiction exists that foundation myths and traditions do not change or even evolve over time. This fiction is understandable, as much is at stake. Because communities are deeply invested in creating stability and preventing chaos, they develop strategies to maintain order. Often, such strategies include the denial of change. Thus, foundation myths derive a considerable amount of their power from the perception that they are ancient and immutable.

But in spite of efforts to halt the process, communities do challenge and reshape basic narratives.[13] Sometimes this is done consciously, and at other times it happens without direct intent. The changes are subtle, taking place over extended time periods. In the short term, Jews retain old stories while simultaneously reinterpreting them to match new circumstances and address new priorities.

Mechanisms for integrating change can be found in Talmudic discussions, where rabbis usually cited a previous teaching or authority as precedent for any innovation they introduced. Major transformations destabilize the social fabric of a community. By invoking precedent, leaders enable communities to feel comfortable with change instead of threatened by it.

Despite resistance to the process, communities do challenge and reshape basic narratives. These changes are discrete and occur over a long period of time. Eventually, after the passage of time and introduction of many changes, communities find themselves with new foundation myths. Each new story sits atop the previous one, forming a palimpsest or multi-layered document.[14] Previous layers (stories) are not discarded, but their significance or position may shift under the preponderance of a new meaning structure.

This shifting is a key point. One foundation story does not eradicate or replace an earlier narrative. The additional narrative augments what has gone before. Just as adding a third dimension to an object does not eliminate the other two dimensions, so changing the dominant story does not erase what has preceded it.

For example, there is abundant rabbinic commentary on the revelation at Sinai. Yet the Bible reports little about this event. The Book of Psalms makes regular reference to the events of the Exodus story but hardly even touches upon Sinai, despite the rabbinic emphasis on the latter. This shift in focus from the Exodus to Sinai illustrates a shift in the dominant foundation story. The Exodus story is neither challenged nor discarded. Rather, the Exodus becomes a part of the Sinai story and is interpreted within this new context. This narrative and interpretative shift reflects significant differences in Jewish circumstances during two different eras.

Another example of a shifting narrative is found in Jewish liturgy after the destruction of the First Temple and the abandonment of the sacrificial system. After the destruction of the Temple, the traditional liturgy still included texts describing prescribed offerings. The mere mention of these offerings reminds readers of the Temple foundation story. However, the context surrounding offerings has completely changed. Not only are sacrifices no longer offered, but the text describing them is now embedded within the wider context of the Torah foundation story.

Thus, we can cite historical precedent for altering the Jewish foundational narrative.[15] In the past, events occurred that were so catastrophic that they completely changed the foundation story of our people and radically transformed Jewish operative ideals, law, observance and practice. Cessation of offerings and the substitution of prayer for sacrifice is but one significant example of a major shift. We are now living in another time of transition that calls for a shift in our master narrative.

After Exodus and Sinai:
A Revised Foundation Story Based on Creation

The whole of Jewish communal life—Jewish law, practice and observance, communal norms and institutions, and events and celebrations—follows from the foundation story and from the application of that story to life.[16] As rabbis who are intimately involved with the lives of people in our communities, it is clear to us that there have been significant changes in our Jewish world. One in particular is the reality that increasing numbers of Jews marry or partner with non-Jews. As part of the search for ways to preserve the continuity of the Jewish story and retain intermarried Jews who are committed to our destiny, we must re-examine our foundation story.

No matter what the era, the central question answered (and asked) in all foundation stories remains the same: "What is the means to redemption?" As we look to answer this question today, we rely on Jewish narratives and their traditional interpretations. We also examine the possibility of an altered narrative.

The first foundation story is the Exodus, a primary, emblematic story of redemption—not only for Jewish people, but also for peoples throughout the world. This story is still told and is included in liturgy and celebration, most notably *Pesach*.

Sinai framed the second major narrative of the Jewish people. Sinai began to take center stage after the destruction of the First Temple (586 BCE). The institution of Torah reading and study created by Ezra (500 BCE) flow from this story.[17] With the advent of Sinai as the primary foundation story, Exodus was understood as the beginning of a process that led to revelation. *Shavuot* was reinterpreted as a Torah-giving holiday, and the road to redemption was posited as the study of Torah and the observance of its teachings. *Halachah* became the means of redemption.[18] The Sinai story now co-existed with the Exodus foundation story.

We propose that the most appropriate foundation story for our modern era is the Creation narrative. From it follows the potential to shape communal decisions based on the value of the individual. Individual worth comes from personal uniqueness and a system that is based on equality. Franz Rosenzweig writes that God's act of creating is the beginning of self-expression. Creation is the granting by God of the opportunity for everyone to find his or her own way in making a unique contribution to the process of redemption.[19] The Creation story is based on the concept that every individual, Jew and non-Jew, is created *b'tzelem Elohim* and has intrinsic worth.[20]

Choosing the Creation narrative as a foundation story for our era does not obviate revelation. Creation values are counter-intuitive in our mass society, obscured by a pervasive attempt to reduce people and ideas to the lowest common denominator. Rabbis, therefore, must rely upon revelation as the basis for authority in implementing Creation values. Revelation provides the footing upon which the efficacy of Creation values rests.

But divine revelation in our time cannot be the same as our first reading of Sinai in Exodus 19-20. One commentator explains that the Sinai story had little impact in the Bible itself. For example, it is hardly mentioned in the Book of Psalms, which constantly refers to the events surrounding the Exodus.[21] The sense of revelation for us is to be found in the *Aleph* of *Anokhi*.[22] It is the divine spark within each one of us.

During our time, redemption is to be transformed to a process, a verb. Redeeming the world is an everyday process of keeping promises and thereby building trust. Redeeming the world means that the values of Creation will lead us to understand that the divine spark inhabits everyone and every aspect of creation. It is the foundation for a Judaism open to participation, to an acceptance of pluralism as both real and as another part of the divine plan.

Non-Jews in Jewish History

As we revise our framework to accommodate the circumstances of contemporary Jewish life in the United States, we find our antecedents in the emergence of modernism in the eighteenth century. During the Age of Reason, the world became more secular. Ghetto walls came down, and Jews enjoyed greater access to and freedom within the world at large. As a result, many Jews found themselves answering to and guided by the state more than by traditional Jewish authority and tradition.

The changes that began in the eighteenth century are amplified and expanded for Jews living in the United States today. Jews now enjoy unprecedented freedom to move easily in a world that is largely open, secular, and rational. Jews also live in a time when individualism dictates modes of behavior far more than does communalism. Jewish participation in a pluralistic, secular world is accompanied by an increasing break from tradition and rabbinic authority.

The tension lies in upholding the communality of Judaism, with its network of obligations and ethical demands, and participating in a secular world which offers apparently limitless means for self-expression. In this modern era, the individual commands. God is seen as manifest in human acts of justice, righteousness, and compassion. We are engaged in creating a new covenant, and like the rabbis in *Bava Metzia* 59a[23], we emphatically proclaimed that revelation, God's intrusion into communal matters, must cease and that responsibility for determining Jewish life falls within the human realm.

But unlike those rabbis, who saw themselves as determining how matters in the human realm were to be handled, we have opened this process up to the Jewish community at large. The current process of decision-making takes into account a great number of determinants, many of them stemming from the attitudes and outlooks of those who make up the *kahal* (community). The covenant has been transformed from obligatory to voluntary. This transformation represents a profound change with a consequent need to reframe our guiding story.

The question of the role and place of non-Jewish people in the context of the Jewish community is not a new one.[24] Biblical literature reflects the self-confidence of a majority culture, one not threatened by its non-Jewish inhabitants. Israelites were taught to protect the *ger toshav*, the "resident alien," with the added reminder to remember that we ourselves were once resident aliens (in Egypt). Israelites were enjoined to treat this vulnerable population with justice and compassion.

We learn of two distinct groups of non-Israelites. First was the *ger toshav* who chose to live among Israelites, assuming the obligations of taxation and obedience to the law. Residence assumed consent to Israelite government as ruling authority. The *ger toshav*'s relationship to the culture was based on mutual obligations.[25] The second group of non-Jews was not part of the culture and did not live among the Israelities. These non-Jews sent delegations when the Temple was dedicated and offered sacrifices. Their voluntary participation in Temple ritual was accepted.[26]

Though the *ger toshav* was under no communal obligation to offer sacrifices, he could voluntarily do so.[27] The exception to this voluntary offering was the paschal celebration.[28] Because the Passover redemptive stories of the Exodus and Temple were not part of the *ger toshav*'s experience, it was deemed inappropriate for the *ger toshav* to fulfill the communal obligations stemming from these.

This entire situation changed when Jews lost their majority status at the time of the first exile and became a minority, often living under hostile conditions. There was mutual distrust and antagonism between Jews and non-Jews during difficult times. Even in the best of situations, Jews were often merely tolerated. The dominant culture's attitude toward Jews was frequently contemptuous. Jewish attitudes in turn were marked by feelings of superiority.[29]

This attitude partially influenced the shift in the redemptive story from the Exodus tale to the Sinai narrative. The Sinai narrative emphasized the exclusive relationship between the Jewish people and God, mirroring a social reality in which Jews were set apart from the dominant culture and forced to look more intensely inward for meaning and validity. In light of both social circumstances and theology, the question of the role of the non-Jew in the Jewish community was moot. In fact, one could say that it remained a silent part of the story until the events of the mid-twentieth century, with the explosion of a Jewish presence in the Diaspora, especially in the United States.

With the secularization of the state and loss of influence of religious institutions at the end of the eighteenth and nineteenth centuries came the universalization of communal obligations. In the Age of Reason, both Jews and non-Jews were citizens of the state. Religious affiliation was secondary. Concomitantly, there was an increase of interpersonal contact between Jews and non-Jews. Attitudes towards Jews and Judaism became more respectful. Intermarriage increased.

Intermarriage and the Jewish Foundation Story

Placing the Creation narrative as the top layer of our foundation story creates a framework for a world in which pluralism and participation co-exist—to the enhancement and enrichment of Judaism. Embracing this model as our current, primary narrative makes it possible to acknowledge that a Jew married to a non-Jew can have a place in the community. It opens a way to validate the commitments made by intermarried families to the history of our people. The alternative is to cast out those who would join their destiny to ours were they permitted to do so. We are guided by a narrative that honors the God of Israel and finds ways to permit God's manifold creatures to dwell inside the Jewish tent.

Both the Exodus and the Sinai foundation stories are exclusive, permitting only certain of God's people to be part of the narrative. The Creation story maintains that we all are God's creatures. It allows us to enlarge the narrative and to find a place for those who are "other."

The Creation story also makes room for us to acknowledge that in this modern era, any community is based on the obligations that people choose to accept. The choice is voluntary, but once inside the community, obligations can be negotiated within the system. Thus, we can still define and maintain those boundaries that we recognize as essential to maintaining Jewish integrity. With Creation as the key paradigm, we assert that redeeming the world entails recognition that the divine spark inhabits everyone and every aspect of creation. It is open to both participation and to pluralism, while not negating boundary maintenance.

In order to flourish, we must recognize that there are people—like the *gerei toshav* of old—linked to our community but not commanded to honor our obligations. To validate their place among us, we need to define these linkages and propose a means by which non-Jews can participate in non-obligatory areas of communal existence.

It is the Jew who experiences most intensely a sense of alienation and rejection when his or her non-Jewish life partner is completely left out of the master story and has no standing within communal structures.

Redefining our guiding foundation story allows us to find valid ways to include intermarried people, Jew and non-Jew, within the synagogue walls and community. By so doing we do not dilute our tradition. Instead, we increase Jewish continuity by finding a place for all of those who would dwell amongst us and share our destiny.

APPENDIX B
Profiles in Intermarriage

In thinking about intermarried households, it is helpful to differentiate between the various understandings such partners have regarding their relationship to Conservative Judaism. The following essays were written by individuals who took part in a study group that ran concurrently with the rabbinic study group that prepared this document. Throughout this time, dialogue between the two groups took place regularly. Everyone profiled here belongs to one of the Conservative synagogues that participated in the *Tiferet* Project.

The narrative stories of intermarried households can be divided into major categories that mirror the major categories into which *k'rovei Yisrael* fit. (Some of these distinctions were delineated in Bruce Phillips' study.)[30] In all of the partnerships represented here, there is agreement on rearing Jewish children without any reservation. There is also commitment to maintaining a Jewish household. While not everyone agrees on what exactly constitutes a Jewish household, we mean a home governed by the cultural and religious norms as they are understood within the immediate synagogue community.

We've identified five categories in which *k'rovei Yisrael* may be placed. The people who write here may be roughly categorized as follows:

♦ Affiliating with another religion but totally committed to rearing Jewish child(ren) and maintaining a Jewish home
♦ Respect for and understanding of Judaism, willingness to support family's Judaism in every way, but a-religious in general orientation
♦ Strong commitment and attraction to Conservative Judaism, but without making final step into conversion (strong "Judeaophile")
♦ Seriously considering conversion
♦ Jews-by-choice; this of course makes the person a Jew—period. This category is included because often it takes awhile for this decision to be made, and the decision is strongly influenced by how the *ger* is treated during that period when he/she is not yet converted.

Each of the eight people who wrote these statements are or were intermarried. Two of the writers are persons who are now Jews. They chose to become Jews after being intermarried for some years. We include these statements to put a human face on intermarriage and to demonstrate who the people are about and for whom this document is written.

Angela Alonso-Bileca When I came to the United States from Spain for graduate work, the furthest thing from my mind was that I would end up living here, married to an American—an American Jew, to be more specific. When I met my future husband, I was glad to see that religion played an important part in his life since religion has always permeated my life. I was brought up Catholic. My parents made religious rituals part of our daily lives, and on Sundays we went to church together. I went to church regularly until the end of my college years, when I did not feel as connected as before to my faith. I still consider myself Catholic and believe in most of the main principles of the Church. My husband, on the other hand, had gone through a religious crisis beginning in his adolescence and lasting until the end of his undergraduate years. He came back to Judaism as a graduate student. His Judaism now has a relevant role in his life, and he is committed to maintaining and strengthening it.

When my husband and I decided to get married, we included both Jewish and Catholic rituals in the ceremony as a sign of mutual respect for our faiths. We talked at length about how to raise our kids, and we both agreed on the importance of a religious education. In fact, neither of us could imagine being brought up without strong ethical guidance. Then came the question of raising the kids Catholic, Jewish or both. We discarded bringing our kids up as hybrids of two religions since we felt it would be confusing for them. We also thought we would end up "watering down" the main principles of each religion. We settled on educating them as Jews, since religion played a more central part in my husband's life than in mine. We were aware that there would be moments of conflict and pain between us because of our religious differences, but we were confident we would get through them with mutual respect and love for our children. I took on the task of educating myself in Judaism, buying challah on Shabbat, learning the prayers, and taking out the *tzedakah* box.

The real challenge was when I became pregnant with my firstborn. Although we had made the commitment to raise our child Jewish, I could not give up the idea of baptizing him as well. I tried to explain to my husband that it was a ritual to welcome life and to sanctify it, and that this was a universal principle. My husband reminded me, sorrowfully, that it was also a ritual to welcome a baby into the Catholic Church, which was something we had agreed not to do. He was right, but there was a lot of pain and sadness in not transferring to my child the ritual my parents used to welcome me into the world and into Catholicism. Furthermore, I was well aware of the pain I would cause my parents when I told them about our decision, although I knew that they would never express their disappointment to me. It was at that time I realized what rearing my kids as Jews would mean. It meant giving up my own memories of moments of joy in rituals, giving up transmitting certain ideas and principles for the sake of keeping a Jewish household and being true to a promise I made to my husband and children.

But what about the promise I made to myself and to the Catholic Church when I was confirmed at sixteen? What about my principles and my Catholic moral base? How was I supposed to reconcile my Catholic upbringing with Judaism?

My solution has been to look at both religions and concentrate on the many ideals and morals that they share. When Judaism and Catholicism differ, I keep my thoughts to myself. In fact, these issues are not a sore point in our marriage since my husband is very respectful of my beliefs. When our children are old enough to understand, I'll tell them that there are festivities important to their mother because they are rituals of her religion, which is not Judaism. If my children ask me about my beliefs I will explain them, but I will also reaffirm their Jewish identity.

Once I was fully aware my son was not going to be baptized, and finally accepted it, having the Jewish rituals of welcoming and conversion was the next appropriate step. We had a *brit*; three months afterwards our son was submerged in the *mikvah* and he will go to religious school until his bar mitzvah. I really enjoyed going through the first two rituals, and I came out of them feeling that I was doing the right thing and feeling, for the first time, comfortable with our decision. When my husband had an *aliyah* in the synagogue with our son, he was the one who held him, read from the Torah, and said the prayers. Because I am not Jewish and have great respect for the sanctity of religious rituals, I sat in the back and watched this ceremony. My husband and some members of the congregation were dismayed that I did not participate in such a key moment in my son's religious life because they knew I was committed to rearing him as a Jew. I, on the other hand, did not feel offended or excluded. I simply felt like a non-Jew who wanted to be respectful of rituals and traditions that are not mine.

Although I still bring the same respectful "backstage" attitude to many of the rituals, I have not been excluded from the life of the synagogue. I have participated in study sessions (especially regarding interfaith marriage), I have enrolled my son in a tot-Shabbat class, I accompany him on Saturdays, I have sponsored *kiddushes*, I meet with some of my *havurah* friends, and I host Shabbat dinners often. I have always felt welcome by the synagogue members, and I have a good relationship with our rabbi, who knows our family quite well. However, I believe my feeling of acceptance may in part be due to the fact that I have consciously not attempted to "rock the boat" or challenge current synagogue practices. Nor have I or my husband become involved in central steering committees. Opportunities for friction thus far have therefore been minimized in my case. However, as my son gets older, and now that we are expecting a second child, I anticipate becoming more active in the regular functioning of our synagogue. I would like to see space made for me—and all committed non-Jewish parents—in appropriate rituals (especially those having to do with lifecycle) and community events.

I also know that few interfaith families in my community have had an experience as pleasant as mine. Some of them have felt ostracized or rejected. Some others were deeply hurt when they could not participate in their children's life rituals; some felt that conversion was the only way to be fully accepted. I would like to raise a voice in their favor. I would like them to be treated as members of the community instead of as second-class citizens. I would like them to be included in rituals that involve their own families, because these non-Jews have provided a Jewish household and Jewish religious education. And I would like the Jewish community to acknowledge that many of these non-Jews had to sacrifice a part of themselves to respectfully commit their children to Judaism.

Dennis Gildea I am a non-Jewish husband in a Jewish household. I grew up in a neighborhood in Los Angeles with many Jewish friends, including my best friend, so I have never seen Jews or Judaism as strange, exotic, or discomforting in any way. When I married a Jew and decided to bring up Jewish children, my only concern was that one day my children would question my views and think less of me because of the decisions I made. But I suppose this is common to all parents, regardless of religion.

The questions came sooner than I expected, "Why aren't you Jewish?" and "If you're not Jewish, why do you go to services?" My answer was that celebrating certain holidays or joining a synagogue is a family decision, but that what a person believes is an individual choice. That seemed to be generally satisfactory, although the parting shot from my six-year-old was "I still don't see why you don't just be Jewish."

I've experienced little difficulty with my choice. I'm not particularly interested in being in a group of people who think just like me, although I recognize that others feel differently about this. My view is that I learn a lot more from people who say, "But what about this?" than from people who say "Right on." I don't expect the congregation to actively celebrate my being different; passive acceptance is perfectly fine with me. I think everyone who knows me at all knows I am not Jewish, but it just doesn't come up much.

We have made a number of good friends through the synagogue. My wife participates on boards and committees as much as she likes, and we attend services and social events without any discomfort.

There was an issue about voting in synagogue elections, which led to a discussion of who should (and by implication who should not be) members. My wife and I disagree on this. My view is that because I am not Jewish, I am not going to tell other people who the next rabbi should be. I do not want to vote on religious issues. Last time it came up, it was very important to my wife that I vote. I had to weigh that against my discomfort with voting, and I did vote for our current rabbi. I reflected on it afterward. Next time, I will not vote on a religious matter. My wife regards the issue as one of "no taxation without representation"—she thinks that if the synagogue takes my money, it should accept my vote. I think this argument holds some weight when applied to fiscal matters at the synagogue, such as deciding on new construction or possibly moving the synagogue, but not for religious matters. Sometimes you have to agree to disagree and just go on.

I did sit through a sermon once at a Reform temple where my in-laws were members, in which the rabbi spoke of interfaith marriage as presenting a "threat of assimilation" to the Jewish people. That was rather off-putting. If I thought that my wife or children were being told that my marriage was wrong or destructive, then we simply would not belong to a synagogue. But I have heard none of that at our synagogue.

What I most want from the Jewish community is for them to make my wife and children happy. My participation in lifecycle events is more important to her than to me.

My wife has a cousin who is a rabbi, so we had no problem getting married in a Jewish ceremony. Our next issue will be our sons' bar mitzvahs in a few years. I understand there are some limitations on my participation in the ceremony, but my wife would like to find a way around these restrictions. At present, however, I do not think I will feel any less proud while watching from the audience. It also came as a surprise to my wife that because I am not Jewish, the rabbi would not be able to officiate at my funeral. That's one service I will have to miss, so it's not of direct interest to me. But I know it will be important to my wife.

Ellen Gobler I was reared as a Conservative Jew in Philadelphia. I attended Hebrew school, was confirmed, attended three summers of Camp Ramah and was a bat mitzvah. My mom still keeps a kosher home. I thought for sure I would marry a Jewish man and have a full Jewish life.

Then I moved to San Francisco in 1996 and became a member of an East Bay Conservative shul. When I met Larry in 1997, I was thirty-six and he was thirty-seven. Before we seriously dated, we discussed my being Jewish and his being a non-practicing Methodist. He agreed to attend courses offered by the shul covering the basics of Judaism. We were married by a female cantor in a Jewish ceremony (we had the seven blessings, *ketubah*, etc.) but with the service in English. Larry has been to family seders, goes with me for Rosh Hashanah and Yom Kippur services, and fasts with me. He has not been to Shabbat services. I am leery about bringing him, and I think he senses it. In the larger picture I am at odds with my level of Jewish involvement right now.

I used to go to shul on Saturdays and feel a bit lost because I did not know anyone. I met a few people and then it was better. After we married, I wanted to do things that brought us closer together. Going to shul alone was not one of them. Now that we have been married for almost five years, I have mentioned to Larry that I feel the need to connect with my faith again. We are also trying to start a family, and that brings up many issues pertaining to our future.

Right now, I avoid the shul because I am afraid I will be "found out," that is, singled out as someone who is married to a non-Jew. I also try to imagine how it would be for my husband to be in a roomful of people as they are singing and chanting in a language he doesn't understand. Fortunately, I know the prayers and tunes by heart, but he struggles with the transliterations and has no knowledge of the content or the reason for any of the prayers. I wouldn't know where to start explaining. I am concerned that if I take him on Shabbat he will not have the luxury of getting lost in the crowd as he does at the High Holidays. I worry that it will not be a positive experience for him. I also fear that it will be very hard for me to feel totally accepted. If I go to shul alone and start meeting people, I will eventually tell them that my husband is not Jewish, and I am sure they will be nice. But what will they really be thinking?

I need to have a path to follow that makes Larry feel he is welcome and takes into account that he is an adult and that Judaism was not part of his life before he met me. I have never expressed an expectation that he convert. It is my best hope that he will embrace some Jewish activities and beliefs, help keep a Jewish home, rear Jewish children and feel my Judaism is something we share. I had hoped the shul would hold my hand through this process. It seems I need to do this work on my own.

In a perfect world, there would be immediate outreach to all interfaith couples/families. A person would ask what things you need to think through tough decisions and give you contacts, information, books, group meetings, and counselor recommendations. Being intermarried is often overwhelming. I don't even know how to start some of these discussions with Larry. This is a place I have never been before in my life; I don't have past experiences to draw upon.

On another level, I am at great odds with my concept of the rabbi and his or her role in my life, in the Conservative synagogue, and in the community. I grew up with rabbis who seemed larger than life. I saw them as direct messengers to God, and I imparted a great deal of power to them. I think that I still carry that image with me today. When I moved here, I loved the shul that I joined and was drawn to the rabbi. He is smart and funny, and I really think he has an intelligent outlook on Judaism. Once I started dating Larry, I withdrew and did not make an effort to make contact with the rabbi. I desperately wanted to talk about my possible future in an interfaith marriage, but I was terrified to speak with him. I feared that he would scold me for not having found a husband within my faith. I thought he'd tell me I'd failed, and that I was less of a Jew for not marrying a Jew. I thought he would judge me and find me unworthy as a Jew. I assumed many negative things that were not necessarily based on reality, but nonetheless seemed real or potentially real.

It broke my heart that I could not approach my rabbi to perform the wedding ceremony and that I could not have an *ufruf* or an *oneg*. It was as if I had a big, fat secret that was keeping me from experiencing some of the most wonderful and fulfilling life events within my shul because of my husband's religious status. I have battled with myself over whether to approach my rabbi to start a dialogue. For the first time in my life as a Jew, I feel on some level as if I am an outcast and that I have "sinned" by marrying outside of the faith.

I have yet to determine how to reconcile these emotions. I long for the time when I was carefree and uninhibited about my faith. There was so much spirit and joy in my Jewish activities in my earlier years. I hope that somehow I can find a safe place in the shul and community to experience this again in the company of my husband.

Alice Hale I recently converted to Judaism after eighteen and a half years of an interfaith marriage, nine years as a mother raising Jewish children, and more than six years as a member of a Conservative synagogue.

The reasons that I converted when I did are many and varied, but I want no one who reads this to be under the impression it was done out of frustration or exasperation. I did not shrug my shoulders after yet another slight and say, "All right, already. I'll convert."

On the contrary, I finally converted because of the warm welcome I have always felt from my Jewish in-laws, and later, the Jewish community I joined. I love and admire these people, and ultimately, I wanted to be like them. My husband's family (immediate and extended) welcomed me unquestioningly. The fellow parents at my daughters' preschool welcomed me as well. The members of the school committee at my synagogue encouraged me to speak up at meetings, even though I didn't grow up going to Hebrew school. My women friends in Hadassah always invited me to meetings. I never felt marginalized. I think all these people recognized that even though I was not Jewish, I had made a commitment to Judaism by joining the synagogue and raising my children as Jews. Though I don't think any of them gave it much thought, they all seemed to recognize that pulling me in, rather than pushing me away, would be better for the community.

Therefore, as my participation, and my husband's, grew, I found I wanted to be more and more involved, particularly in the ritual aspects of Judaism. I was very honored at High Holidays to be asked to read one of the English prayers after the Torah service. I found myself wishing, however, that I could have a "real" honor. It was at that point that I realized that I wanted to become Jewish. Ritual had come to mean enough to me that I wanted to be able to be able to fully participate, and because I was given many opportunities to learn more about Judaism, I came to understand why I couldn't as a non-Jew.

But even if I had been allowed to do these things (have an *aliyah*, read the Torah, etc.), as a non-Jew, they would have been shallow and devoid of meaning because I knew the reasoning behind them. I am a traditional type, and I understand that rituals have meaning. Why perform them if you are undermining the meaning?

While I was undergoing the process of conversion, some controversy arose in our synagogue (generated within the board of directors, and having nothing to do with our new rabbi) about the status of non-Jewish spouses in the congregation. Were they members? Could they vote, serve on committees, chair a committee? Rather than making me want to convert faster, I am afraid that this debate put a damper on my enthusiasm for embracing Judaism. Could this community that I love really become as mean-spirited as some members sounded? I was especially bothered because I could see no problems that the current, rather benign approach to non-Jewish spouses had caused. It seemed to be an arbitrary act of exclusion to suddenly want to enumerate all the things we "shouldn't" do, especially as they had nothing to do with ritual.

Fortunately, this blew over with few repercussions, though I know it did damage some relationships and led to bitter feelings on the part of some intermarried Jews. When I was satisfied that it was an isolated event, I felt better about continuing with my plans to convert.

When the *Tiferet* group was formed, about the time I had started to prepare for my conversion, I wanted to participate even though I knew that by the end of the year we would no longer be an interfaith family. My participation in the group was driven by a desire to encourage acknowledgement of interfaith families by the institutions of Conservative Judaism. When I go to the United Conservative Synagogues website, I am frustrated, and offended by the concentration on "getting the kids to date other Jews." As a parent, I would love it if my daughters would someday marry Jewish men. But even more important, I want them to marry men who are ethical, kind, caring and will love them. If they aren't Jewish, but have all those other qualities, who am I to be disappointed?

Besides, realistically, the world has moved beyond "How do we get the kids to date other Jews?" The kids are not only dating non-Jews, they are marrying them and having children. Many of them desire some kind of Jewish home life. It is no longer a debate of "should they or shouldn't they?" They have, and the question is, "How are we going to deal with this?" If we don't find a way, many intermarrieds will say "Okay, you want us to go away, fine. But we'll take our Jewish spouses and our potentially Jewish children with us, and I doubt we will ever come back."

Those of us who make up the non-Jewish half of these couples want it recognized that choosing to raise our children in another faith represents a sacrifice and loss on our part. We have not made the choice lightly, and we are not asking for consideration out of a desire to damage Judaism or Jewish institutions. We are asking to be included because being excluded is painful. Parents who drive to Hebrew school, help at the Purim carnival, and go to the Share-A-Shabbat dinner don't want to be on the *bimah* at a bar mitzvah just to make trouble. They want their participation in their children's religious education—their children's lives—to be recognized. It hurts to learn that after giving so much, you can still be cut of the process.

Rabbis: Welcome interfaith couples into your congregation. Talk to them, explain things, meet with them, encourage them, and even invite them to participate in congregational activities to the greatest extent possible. The very fact that they are in your congregation is a huge gesture indicating they want some kind of Jewish home life—more so than for some in-married Jewish couples. I doubt any interfaith couple joins a Conservative synagogue casually, and they deserve to be dealt with honestly and frankly. If the Conservative community they've chosen is not a good fit, they should find that out sooner rather than later.

Even if you are disturbed by intermarriage, resist the urge to be judgmental and disapproving. Few things are more painful—or harder to forgive—than being told that the most intimate and important relationship of your life is misguided, destructive or will lead to "cultural genocide." (As an intermarried trans-racial adoptive mother, I know whereof I speak.)

Even after a conversion, some of these issues will continue to emerge. Times have changed from the days when an intermarriage meant the end of a relationship with one set of relatives. That's a good thing. But intermarriage requires some imagination and flexibility on the part of the family and their religious community to make the children of that family feel they can embrace different aspects of their culture. My children will always have non-Jewish relatives and a non-Jewish heritage. I hope that their Jewish community will never make them feel less Jewish because of it.

I recently read in the Jewish press an article entitled "Our Grandparents' Story." It went on to describe the arrival of Eastern European immigrants to the Upper East Side of New York. Well, that's not my grandparents' story—nor my children's. For years I said I wouldn't convert because I couldn't convert to the culture. I finally realized that I could become a part of the religion, and the culture, while bringing my own background and heritage to the mix. I would hope the Jewish community learns to help others do the same.

David C. Jeffrey Before I begin, a disclaimer: My non-conversion is in no way a negative reflection on Judaism. I am involved with the Jewish people. I share their joys and consider their problems mine. Rather, I am trying to show that respect for Judaism is a complex thing and can be expressed in different ways.

I was brought up in Scotland, a place where the number of Jews was so small that I saw them as ancient and exotic, not as a living people. What little I knew about Jews came from the Bible, Shakespeare, and in parallel, a growing awareness of the indescribable horrors of the Holocaust. As I traveled to other places, however, I gradually formed a fuller, more detailed picture of the Jewish people. I became aware of the many who have made major contributions to science and culture, a disproportionately large gift to humanity for such a small community. I finally moved to California, and my personal journey of discovery reached its climax with my choice of a Jew as life partner.

My life partner is a very committed Jew. She was a founding member of her Conservative synagogue and still plays an active part in it. She is observant to the extent of keeping our kitchen kosher and more. For my part, as a child I had been exposed to the Church of Scotland's very Puritan brand of Christianity. But as soon as my parents permitted me to "opt out," I did so. Since then I have had no connection to, or interest in, religion. In fact, I took a definite stance against organized religion, on the grounds of its intolerance and involvement in, and even responsibility for, many horrifying episodes in history.

However, my partner felt that for me to understand her more fully it was important that I understand more about Judaism. So, under the auspices of her synagogue, she created a study group for intermarried couples. For the last four years we have been studying and celebrating together. I feel I now know more about Judaism than I ever expected to know of any religion.

Amongst the things I learned early on is that being an observant Jew means living by Jewish law, one of whose major prohibitions is against marrying a non-Jew. (A stigma attaches to those who disregard this rule by marrying non-religious Scotsmen!) I learned that there are certain activities, particularly in shul, which are closed to non-Jews. I also learned that conversion was possible, even for someone like me, and that I had a strong reason to consider it. By converting I would restore my partner's position in the community (quite apart from any personal benefits).

So why don't I convert? Here is my personal reply. I have two basic reasons for not converting, and they are connected with the dual nature of "Jewish": the religious, Judaic component, and the peoplehood, or tribal, component. I am aware that Jews prefer to minimize this distinction, feeling that they are two inseparable halves to the Jewish whole, and I know that it is impossible to convert and become a secular Jew.

Nevertheless, I perceive "Jewishness" as having two parts. Taking the Judaic component first: In spite of all I have learned about Judaism, I remain an atheist. My rational mind has problems with the notion that there is some kind of Supreme Being, let alone one who has time to listen (and respond) to individual prayer. Interestingly, it has become clear to me that this view is shared by many religious people, including my partner, who nevertheless continue their religious observance. Belief brings something very important to their lives, even though rational thought is often at variance with spiritual attitudes. ("Living with contradiction," I understand, is very Jewish!)

I use the word "spiritual" here with some trepidation, as it is very loaded: it is my way of referring to the drive to religious activity or belief. This is a drive I personally don't feel. Friends have said of me that I lack the "religious bone." If I possess this drive, it must take some form of which I am unaware. During religious discussions I feel a bit like a blind man having color described to him. At some fundamental level I "don't get" religion, including Judaism. What being with my partner has changed for me is that I now (late in life) have a better appreciation of how complex religion is and how important it can be to people. I now see the positive side of what I had previously dismissed. But I could never convert without a proper understanding of religion. It would make me feel a hypocrite. I would not be treating Judaism with respect.

Secondly, there is what I call the tribal component. I now have the privilege of knowing many Jews, religious and non-religious. I have become aware of their common characteristics, distinctive traits I find attractive (for the most part), but characteristics very different from mine. Jews tend to have a shared set of values, world views and cultural backgrounds which shapes who they are. The expression (which I'm afraid I have often heard describing a convert) "You can hardly tell they weren't born a Jew" strengthens the view that the only way to be really Jewish is to be born a Jew. My background is hugely different, and the idea that I could become "Jewish" without a lifetime's effort seems ludicrous. And, to me, this is perfectly fine. I think one of the great riches of the world we inhabit is the variety of cultures, customs and peoples.

It is for these reasons that I am not presently considering conversion. I hope that a Jew reading this will appreciate my respect for Judaism. The temptation to convert simply to make life easier exists, and I know people who have done it. To my mind, however, it doesn't make them Jews in any real sense, and I can't see that Judaism gets anything other than a statistical boost from such conversions.

Finally, a plea: the history of the last (and previous) centuries certainly justifies Jewish feelings of paranoia, but the idea that "who is not one of us is against us" is an oversimplification. Not all non-Jews are anti-Semitic. I know several other people like me. They are non-Jews as respectful of Jewish culture and tradition as many Jews, but for their own reasons don't undergo conversion. Yet this seems to be the only act open to us that would gain Jewish trust. I would like there to be some other, less extreme, mechanism that would be accepted as proof of our goodwill to the Jewish people, and (ideally) render us acceptable mates to our Jewish partners.

Mary Kelly Twenty years ago, as Larry and I were driving home after a relative's bar mitzvah, we had a terrible fight about the religious upbringing of our hypothetical children. I was just making conversation when I asked Larry if he expected to have a bar mitzvah should we have a child. "But of course," he said. I replied that in that case I expected to have first communion, confirmation, and any other relevant Catholic rituals. Larry went rigid with rage, jammed on the accelerator, and got pulled over by the highway patrol a short while later for going at an unbelievable speed.

Months later, when we'd calmed down enough to talk about it, we concluded that we'd expose our kids to those pieces of various religious traditions that we thought had some value and let them reach their own conclusions. However, when Willa was born in 1985, I realized that part of the purpose of religious ceremonies around life events like birth is to celebrate the event, to underscore its magic. So we began talking about what to do to honor Willa's birth. Baptism was out. I have not practiced Catholicism since age eighteen. (The argument in the car was really about territory rather than religion). A new age/hippie event didn't fit. The most attractive ceremony to me was from the African-American saga *Roots*, when the father takes his newborn to the mountain, holds her up to the stars and says "Behold the universe, the only thing greater than you are." But that wasn't our tradition either.

Larry thought it would be possible to have Willa named in a synagogue without actually having her converted, and that seemed appealing. I became accustomed to the idea as he researched it. When he found that she would, indeed, have to be converted, I'd become comfortable with the notion. I realized that our Jewish community included poets and stock-brokers, psychologists and drop-outs, Buddhists and atheists. I thought that having a coherent set of values that I respected was a good idea.

So first Willa, and later her sister Lila, was converted before a *bet din* at the University of Judaism. Though a Reform synagogue might have been a better match, Larry thought his family would be appalled if we joined one. Later, we went to a local Conservative synagogue for the High Holidays and *yartzeit*, and we joined when Willa was ready for pre-school. Though other interfaith families warned me that they had experienced prejudice at the synagogue, I haven't had that experience. Once, early on, someone said to me "What kind of a name is Kelly?" I didn't feel offended by the question. I thought that the woman who asked was simply looking for information since Kelly is not a usual name within the synagogue community.

I think it helps that Larry does a great *haftorah* and has been active on the synagogue's board of trustees. Many people have suggested that I convert. But religion in my mind is about God, and I don't have an experience of God. I don't exactly disbelieve. I've just never had a moment where I said, "That's God." I love the community and have become friendly with a number of the people at the synagogue. They were very solicitous of me when the congregation recently rejoined United Synagogue. They did not want me to feel marginalized. I have always felt a little bit different from groups that I have been a part of. At the synagogue I know I'm different and this certainty is comfortable. The community has been a great support when we've hit rough spots. My daughters feel very much at home there. Willa, our eldest, has just graduated from the local *midrasha*, and her younger sister Lila looks forward to continuing her studies there.

Billi Romain Converting to Judaism has been about changing my personal identity—not from one religion to another—but moving from the experience of being an outsider to an insider, from one who feels little sense of belonging to one who belongs to something. And what a something! Judaism is a complex mix of ethnicity, culture, politics, philosophy, spirituality . . . not to mention religion. It's a lot to take on.

As an unofficial part of the synagogue community for almost five years, I have watched both my children engage in religious school and embrace Jewish practices at home. I have tried to understand my husband's ambivalence towards aspects of Conservative Judaism while maintaining that it is the only service that resonates for him. During that time, I have experienced moments of enlightenment, as well as alienation. Most importantly, I have had the pleasure of meeting wonderful people who are committed to spiritual and moral inquiry. I wished to join them.

While my mother is Catholic and my father is Jewish, I was raised with no formal religious education. We celebrated the dominant American holidays, such as the coming of Santa Claus and the Easter Bunny. Even after my parents divorced, my mother made sure we had invitations to attend Passover seders. I was aware that I did not "qualify" as either Christian or Jew. Since I was not baptized, my Christian friends reminded me that I could not go to heaven. At the same time, with a non-Jewish mother, I knew I was not recognized as a Jew.

From an early age, I realized that any relationship I was going to have with my nascent sense of God was going to have to be on my own terms. When I was in first grade, I remember hoping that God would hear my prayers despite my disqualifications. After all, I reasoned, what about all those millions of innocent Buddhist babies? Didn't God care for us as well as them? As an adult, I was drawn to Unitarian Universalism as a community that explored the universal principles of all religions. I found, however, that what this community provided in tolerance and acceptance, it lacked in depth and tradition. I realized then that being a little bit of everything can feel like a lot of nothing.

When I met my husband, Doug, I was glad that he felt a connection to a religious community. We committed to raising our children Jewish because of that connection. Having experienced the "U-Pick'Em" path to religion, I knew I didn't want that for our children. I think that religion works best as something to grow around, as a support structure that helps shape and bind one's moral development. Children can experience religion where adults discern and analyze. It is difficult for me to appreciate rituals through an adult lens that seeks the consistent and rational. Traditions are best recorded by a child's eyes. I love to watch my children basking in the warm glow of the Shabbat candles, blowing the *shofar*, or acting out the exodus at a seder. I feel like these moments are gifts they will own for the rest of their lives.

As I have pursued taking on a religious identity that is consistent with my values, I have come up against the difficulty of simultaneously honoring and owning my Polish heritage. My mother was born in Poland, in the area known during the partition as Galicia. She experienced the horrors of the Second World War in a Soviet slave labor camp. Because my grandfather was in the Polish army, my grandmother and mother were taken to Siberia when Stalin invaded Poland. My grandmother credits the kindness of fellow Jewish prisoners, many of whom bribed their way onto trains to escape the approaching Nazis, with saving their lives. When my eight-year old mother arrived in Chicago, her best friends were Jewish refugees. With them, she shared language, food and culture, in addition to substantial physical and emotional trauma. The first and second generation Polish Americans in her neighborhood were more inclined to ridicule than befriend a peasant girl who spoke broken English and had spent the past five years in refugee camps from Pakistan to Mexico. She grew up an outsider in the Polish community and even pretended to be Jewish in high school in order to fit in. I inherited that sense of alienation, hiding my Polish heritage to avoid being the butt of jokes so popular in suburban Connecticut where I was raised.

Becoming a part of the Jewish community and confronting the roots of my lost past have allowed me to explore what it means to be of Polish descent. As I have tried to integrate these dual identities, I find myself in a cross-cultural study of difficult histories. The full-scale destruction of European Jewry that occurred in Poland during the Holocaust eclipsed the rich and inextricably linked history shared by Jews and Poles. Poland was one of the most important centers of Jewish life in the world. Nearly three quarters of the world's Jews lived in the Polish-Lithuanian Commonwealth in the mid-17th century. This history has been overshadowed by mutual resentment and mistrust in the aftermath of the Holocaust, resulting in a highly charged dialogue between Poles and descendants of Polish Jews.

As I accept myself and identify with my dual heritage, I have felt tension within the Jewish community. I commonly hear diatribes against "the Poles" when I mention that I am of Polish descent. It has felt awkward—almost mutually exclusive—to be both Polish and Jewish.

The process of converting to Judaism has presented practical, as well as existential difficulties. As much as I wanted to convert in my own rhythm when I was ready, it was very difficult being a lower-caste, non-member of the synagogue. About a year ago, a member of the synagogue board informed me that despite a recent invitation, I could not co-chair the social action committee because I was "not Jewish." At that point, I was in the process of studying for conversion, attended services weekly, and had two children enrolled in religious school. I felt like someone had slapped me across the face. I seriously questioned why I would want to join a community that would rather not perform acts of social good than have me co-chair a committee. I left shul early that day and walked home in a downpour. With tears and rain running down my burning cheeks, I realized I would either have to quit or convert. I could no longer tolerate being an outsider.

Why not just quit? I could go to a Reform synagogue where I might even be considered "Jewish-enough." First there was my family to think of. My children enjoy their religious programs and have made wonderful friendships. My husband feels very comfortable with the Conservative services. I had begun to share his appreciation of the beauty with which the synagogue community prays together, the participatory nature of the services and the serious level of inquiry of the congregants.

The process of conversion has been a blessing. Reading and studying with the rabbi has opened my mind and my heart, allowing me to cultivate a sense of *kavanah* (concentration) in prayer and in the everyday. It has required my taking an active role to become something, no longer remaining on the periphery. Studying Torah gives me the opportunity to suspend belief and judgment in search of deeper meaning. The rabbi has assured me that my struggles, questions and doubts are not only allowed in Judaism, but that they are a prerequisite. I look forward to being a full-fledged member of the synagogue and to further investigate what it means to be Jewish.

Katherine Trow To explain my relationship to Judaism, I must first talk about my relationship to Jews. Brought up Protestant in the Midwest, my first sustained contact with Jews came in the state college in Ohio I attended in the late forties. I had Jewish friends on the same floor of our dorm, but *de facto* segregated sororities and fraternities limited our social contacts outside the dorm. "Inter-dating" was rare. Later when I went to work in a private liberal arts and socially/politically liberal college in Ohio, I became close to the many Jewish students and faculty there. It was the same witty, bright and outrageously funny traits in those people that I found in my Jewish college friends that attracted me to them—except this time the Jews were as accessible as the non-Jews. This was also true in the academic community at Berkeley to which I moved in the late fifties. So it was no surprise to me that I dated several Jewish men and eventually chose to marry one. I had always assumed we would raise Jewish children, and this matter was never in dispute.

What surprised me was how seriously my husband-to-be took Judaism, more so than any other of our Jewish friends. He introduced me to Judaism by inviting me to keep him company at services and seders at Hillel. (This was in the early sixties, with no Conservative shul in our community.) He answered my many questions about this exotic religion, so strange and different from the one in which I had been brought up. I was never asked to convert, for he felt that it should come from me. I had long since given up any connection with Christianity in any form, but as a non-believer I did not feel I could convert to any other religion.

From the beginning we maintained a Jewish home. We observed Shabbat and the holidays and festivals, and contributed to Jewish charities. But there was a problem. My husband was never comfortable with any of the Reform services we attended, although I was made to feel welcome in some of them. As he had been raised in a Conservative home, it was only when a local Conservative shul was founded that he felt truly and joyously at home. Although by this time our children had grown, they sometimes attended High Holiday services with us, and we signed up as family members. I believed I was a full synagogue member as no one told me otherwise.

Over the years, I had become painfully aware of the intense objections many Jews had to marrying out. When we read the notice about the formation at our shul of a group for intermarried couples, I was moved to tears. At last someone was recognizing the deep connection to Judaism and Jewishness that many non-Jews in intermarriages have. As an adult, I had always felt myself affiliated to Jews as a people, and I felt assimilated to Jewish culture. Actually my experience was the reverse of the "myth of the *shiksa*" luring the Jew away from his religion, for it was I who felt strongly that we should join the intermarried group to learn more about Judaism. And unexpectedly, through the process of exploring different Jewish themes alongside me, my husband has become more interested and involved in Jewish studies. I found an outlet in the group for my intense feelings of caring about Jews even though I was not one of them. Studying aspects of Judaism helped to fill what I realized was a kind of spiritual vacuum. And with a cohort of similar couples, I no longer felt as isolated.

It came as a complete shock to find out eventually that I was not considered to be a full member of the shul even though we were asked to assume the same financial responsibilities (including dues and contributions to the building fund) as others. The founding and support of the intermarried group, the *Tiferet* Project and open forum, a few meetings with the ritual committee, and the accessibility of the rabbi and other shul officers have made my situation easier and helped to mitigate my feeling of exclusion.

To find a comfortable place within the tent of Conservative Judaism, however, I would like to be recognized for what I am: a non-religious non-Jew who nevertheless has a deep respect for Judaism. I live in a committed forty-three-year-old year relationship. From the beginning I established a Jewish home with my Jewish partner, becoming what the sociologist Bruce Phillips would call a "Judaic family." I believe Conservative Judaism must recognize the role of the non-Jew in helping to create and to sustain these Judaic families. With an eagerness to raise their children as Jews, they need to be made to feel welcome in the synagogue community and to have their children accepted completely as Jews. Any form of exclusion, such as demanding conversion before children may take part in certain activities, is a slap in the face of these Jewish families and denies enhancement of the children's Jewish education and experience. In addition, all the members of such families should be brought "under the tent" when it comes to such practices as baby-naming and *b'nai mitzvot*. Recognizing the need to include non-Jewish family members in these lifecycle practices strengthens Conservative Judaism and helps to prevent the leaching away of intermarried Jews to Reform Judaism or to no Judaism at all.

Conversion is not an active issue for me. My feelings have always been that no matter how close I feel to the Jewish people, I cannot ever become a Jew in a religious sense. My formal religious background has been completely extinguished by my earlier disillusioning experience with Christianity. For me to go through the conversion process would be false and require that I tell untruths. An early, emotionally devastating visit to Yad Vashem reinforced my personal commitment to standing with the Jewish people while not actually being able to become one of them. These are my personal boundaries, and to violate them would be false to my sense of personal identity.

I think of myself as standing steadfastly beside the Jewish people, like Ruth who said, "Whither thou goest, I will go," for as long as I live.

APPENDIX C
Glossary

The terms and definitions listed below were used during the Tiferet Project's deliberations and appear throughout this document.

aliyah (*aliyot*, pl.)   going up to the Torah

bediavad   "it having been done," indicating a situation where an action is being considered after it has taken place, as opposed to *lechatchila* (*ab initio*), where the action is being considered before it has taken place

beit din   rabbinic court of law

bimah   pulpit

b'racha   blessing

chevra kadisha   burial society

chumash (*chumashim*, pl.)   Biblical readings for Shabbat and holidays

drash   (commentary)

ger toshav   a resident alien in biblical times who accepted some of the laws of Judaism

halachah   "the way," Jewish law

hava'at shalom   a positive commandment to bring peace between people—between individuals, between spouses, between and among families, between communities and nations of the world

hi'uv   an obligation to perform an act required by Jewish law; required of a Jew, but not of someone who is not Jewish

kahal   community

kavod   "honor," "respect," "reverence," "importance," "distinction," or "glory," an inclusive term with social, moral and theological implications

k'rov Yisrael (*k'rovei Yisrael*, pl.)   a relative or friend of Israel; a person close to the Jews; a non-Jew who participates in the life of the Conservative synagogue

k'vod habriyot   "respect for people," concept informing *halachic* decisions in a number of areas, including relaxing certain rabbinic restrictions in circumstances where their fulfillment would cause an infringement of a person's dignity *k'vod hatzibbur*   "respect for the community"

kibud av v'em   honoring one's father and mother

lifnim mishurat hadin   going beyond the letter of the law

lechatchila   "ab initio, from the beginning," indicating a situation where an action is being considered before the action has been taken, as opposed to *bediavad*, where the action is considered after it has taken place

lifecycle events   those events such as births, deaths, marriages, which are accompanied by ritual celebrations

mara d'atra   "teacher of this place," the rabbi of the local community, who holds the final authority for making decisions of Jewish law and is empowered by his/her community to do so

ma'arit ayin   "how things appear," used when rabbis prohibit permissible actions because they might be mistaken by an observer for prohibited conduct; used to prevent people from unjustifiably suspecting others of misconduct; also used to forestall the inferences that forbidden actions are permissible

minhag   a post-biblical religious custom, often introduced by a rabbinic authority or based on biblical writ which became binding and assumed the force of law; one of the formative factors in the development of Jewish law and religious observance, including customs that exist in one locality only; customs less binding than formal legal enactments, although some can have the force of law in event of conflict or crisis

minhag hamakom   local practice; binding according to rabbinic law upon natives of the land and those who take up residence there

mipnei darchei shalom   "the ways of peace," referring to many rabbinic enactments instituted to foster peace and to prevent strife and controversy

mitzvah (mitzvot, pl.)   "commandment"

motzei acharim   relieving another Jew of an obligation; for example, responding "amen" when another is required to recite a blessing

shalom bayit   "peace in the house," domestic harmony; reason for many rabbinic decisions, referring to individual home and community at large

shealot u'teshuvot   "questions and answers, *responsa*," method of determining Jewish law through posing questions and eliciting rabbinic responses

sheva mitzvot b'nai Noah   the seven commandments incumbent upon the children of Noah, required of Jews and non-Jews alike in Jewish law; includes prohibitions against idolatry, blaspheming God's name, murder, incest, stealing, and eating limbs off a living animal along with obligation to establish courts of law

siddur   (*siddurim*, pl.) prayerbook

siyag   fence

tiferet   beauty, from the *kabalah* (mythical tradition); unites the opposing forces of strength and kindness

T'shuvot   body of literature composed of rabbinic responses to questions of Jewish law

tumah   "unfitness," *halachic* concept, unrelated to hygiene, that is the antithesis of *tahor*, ritual fitness

REFERENCES

General

Artson, Bradley Shavit. "Facing Intermarriage," *Conservative Judaism*, Winter 1992: 8, 18-19.

Building the Faith: A Book of Inclusion for Dual Faith Families, An Initiative of the Federation of Jewish Men's Clubs.

Cohen, Shaye J.D. "Crossing the Boundary and Becoming a Jew," *Harvard Theological Review* 82:1 (1989): 13-33.

Fisher, Adam D. "*Ger toshav* and Mixed Marriage," *Reconstructionist* May 1973: 22-6.

Greenberg, Steve. "Between Intermarriage and Conversion: Finding a Middle Way," InterfaithFamily.com

Jacob, Walter, editor. *American Reform Responsa*, CCAR Press, 1983

Jacob, Walter 1986. "Participation of Non-Jews in a Jewish Public Service" Editor Contemporary American Reform Responsa, CCAR Press, 1987

161. "Gentiles in a Jewish Congregation"

162. "Congregational Membership for a Non-Jewish Spouse"

163. "Gentile Chairman of Confirmation Group"

165. "May a Non-Jew Light the Shabbat Eve Candles?"

Kelman, Stuart. "A Letter to the Committee on Jewish Law and Standards," June 1, 1999.

Leadership Council of Conservative Judaism. "Statement on Intermarriage," March 7, 1995.

Proceedings of the Committee on Jewish Law and Standards/1980-1985

Abelson, Kassel. "The Non-Jewish Spouse and Children of a Mixed Marriage in the Synagogue," 129-41

Agus, Jacob B. "The *Mitzvah* of *Keruv*," 144-50

Roth, Joel and Daniel Gordis. "*Keruv* and the Status of Intermarried Families," 151-7

Siegel, Seymour. "Comments on *Keruv* and the Status of Intermarried Families," 159-61

Sky, Harry Z. "The *Mitzvah* of *Keruv*," 163-7

——"Should a Non-Jewish Spouse Be a Member of an Affiliate Organization?" p. 134

——"Should Membership in a Christian Church Make a Difference?" p. 134

——"What Role Should a Non-Jewish Spouse Play in the Life Cycle Ritual?" pp.134-5

——"Should a Non-Jewish Spouse Participate in a *Brit* or Naming Ceremony?" p. 135

——"What Role Should a Non-Jewish Spouse Play in a Bar/Bat Mitzvah Ceremony?" pp. 135-6

——"What Role Should a Non-Jewish Parent Play in a Wedding?" p. 136

——"May a Non-Jew Wear a Tallit?" pp. 136-7

——"May a Non-Jewish Spouse Be Buried in a Synagogue Cemetery?" pp. 137-8

——"May Jewish Offspring Recite Kaddish in Memory of a Non-Jewish Parent?" p. 138

——"What is the Status of the Offspring of a Mixed Marriage?" pp. 138-9

——"Before Conversion, May Such Children Attend a Synagogue School?" p. 139

——"Should a Child of a Mixed Marriage (Where the Mother is Non-Jewish) Be Allowed to Join USY? The Synagogue Singles Group?" pp. 139-40

Proceedings of the 2000 Convention

Perkins, Carl M. "The Challenges and Appeals of *Keruv* in a Conservative Context," 292ff.

Regev, Uri and Adam Shear. "Who is a Jew? Legal, Ideological, and Halakhic Dilemmas: Source Materials" (presented at the Conference for the Advancement of Jewish Education, 2001).

Responsa of the Committee on Jewish Law and Standards / 1991-2000
Bergman, Ben Zion "YD 268:1993 The Case of the Unconverted Spouse," 127-31
"YD 367:1.1991. A Matter of Grave Concern: A Question of Mixed Burial,"418-25

Epstein, Jerome M. "EH 16:1993 The Role of the Non-Jewish Parent in the Blessing for Bar/Bat Mitzvah," 603-7

"Issues Regarding Employment of an Intermarried Jew by a Synagogue or Solomon Schechter Day School," 608-11

Responsa on Jewish Cemeteries, Rabbis Diamond, Mark, Gordon Freeman, and Stuart Kelman, May 14, 1993.

Wertheimer, Jack. "Surrendering to Intermarriage," *Commentary* March 2001.

Web Sites

Jewish Outreach Institute: http://www.joi.org
InterfaithFamily: http://www.interfaithfamily.com

NOTES

1. National Jewish Population Survey 2000-01: Strength, Challenge and Diversity in the American Jewish Population. A United Jewish Communities Report in cooperation with the Mandell L. Berman Institute–North American Jewish Data Bank, September 2003.

2. The seven *mitzvot* incumbent upon the children of Noah, required of Jews and non-Jews alike in Jewish law, include prohibitions against idolatry, blaspheming God's name, murder, incest, stealing, and eating limbs off a living animal along with obligation to establish courts of law.

3. See *Genesis* 2:19.

4. See, for example, Rabbi Harry Z. Sky, "The *Mitzvah* of *Keruv*," published by the Committee on Jewish Law and Standards, 1980-1985; see also Rabbi Steve Greenberg's "Between Intermarriage and Conversion: Finding a Middle Way," published on interfaithfamily.com., Oct. 2001.

5. Bernadette J. Brooten, "'Iael prostates' in the Jewish Donative Inscription from Aphrodisias," in *The Future of Early Christianity: Festschrift for Helmut Koester.* Ed. Birger Pearson, et al. [Minneapolis: Fortress, 1991], 149-162.

6. Rabbi Jerome M. Epstein, "Issues Regarding Employment of an Intermarried Jew by a Synagogue or Solomon Schecter Day School," Committee on Jewish Law and Standards, Sept., 1997 (as printed in the *JTS Magazine*, v. 7, n. 6, Spring, 1998).

7. See Shaye J. D. Cohen, *The Beginnings of Jewishness: Boundaries, Varieties, Uncertainties* [Berkeley: University of California Press, 1999].

8. Robert MacIver, *The Web of Government* [New York: Macmillan Company, 1947]. See also Neil Gillman, "The Problematics of Myth," *Sh'ma*, January, 2002.

9. Max Kaddushin, *The Rabbinic Mind* [New York: Blaisdell Publishing Company, 1965].

10. "Israelite Society in Transition," *Etz Hayim* [Philadelphia: The Jewish Publication Society, 2001], 1348-1352.

11. Gordon M. Freeman, *The Heavenly Kingdom* [Lanham, MD: University Press of America, 1986], 59.

12. Ibid, pp. 144ff.

13. Jacob Neusner, *From Politics to Piety* [Englewood Cliffs, NJ: Prentice-Hall, 1973], 2f.

14. A palimpsest occurs when a manuscript's inscription has been erased and another inscription applied. The previous inscription(s) can still be detected and sometimes even recovered. An example is found in the language of the Creation story, *Genesis* 1:2, where the word *t'hom* is used to refer to an abyss whereas the word actually echoes the Babylonian Enuma Elish myth which features the goddess Tiamat. The previous reference (Tiamat in Babylonian lore) has been erased and replaced by *t'hom*. We can still detect the original reference. Previous layers

(stories) are not discarded, but their significance or position may shift under the preponderance of a new meaning structure.

15. Gordon M. Freeman, *The Heavenly Kingdom,* op cit p. 3
16. Gordon M. Freeman, "Israelite Society in Transition," *Etz Hayim,* op cit.
17. *Nehemiah* 8
18. Jacob Neusner, *There We Sat Down* [Nashville, TN: Abingdon Press, 1972], 55 ff.
19. Franz Rosenzweig, *The Star of Redemption,* translated by William Hallo, The Littman Library of Jewish Civilization, 1984, 113.
20. *Genesis* 1:27
21. See Jon Levinson, *Sinai and Zion* [Minneapolis: Winston Seabury, 1985].
22. Gordon M. Freeman, "On Translating Our Heritage into Contemporary Language," in *Proceedings of the Rabbinical Assembly,* 1994, 167-171.
23. Bavli 59a
24. The issue of the relation of Israelites to non-Israelites began in the Bible. See Joel Rembaum, "Dealing with Strangers: Relations with Gentiles at Home and Abroad," *Etz Hayim,* op cit, 1377-1382. See also Shaye J. D. Cohen, op cit.
25. Rembaum, op cit.
26. *I Kings* 8:41-43
27. *Bamidbar* 15:14-16
28. *Exodus* 12:48
29. Howard Sachar, *The Course of Modern Jewish History* [New York: Dell Publishing Company, 1958], 66f, 139.

About the Authors

Mark Bloom joined Temple Beth Abraham of Oakland, California as its rabbi in July of 2001. A native of the Bay Area, he often describes the experience as a "homecoming." Previously, Rabbi Bloom served pulpits in Cranston, Rhode Island; South Salem, New York and Sydney, Australia. He was ordained at the Hebrew Union College in Cincinnati, Ohio, in 1995, and received both Bachelors and Masters Degrees in Communication Studies from Northwestern University in Evanston, Illinois. Rabbi Bloom is especially well-known for his work with children, and is the author of Out of the Mouths of Babes: What Children Can Teach Us About Spirituality, Jewish Issues and the Jewish People. He is also an accomplished songleader, having led groups of all ages throughout the country. Before becoming a rabbi, he worked in advertising for the Clorox Company. He has been married to his wife Karen since 1994 and has two children, Micah and Jonah.

Rabbi Ted Feldman began his service as executive director of Jewish Family and Children's Services of the East Bay in December 1995. Prior to that, he was the executive director of the Jewish Federation of the Sacramento region. Before coming to California, in 1992, he was the campaign director for the South Palm Beach County Jewish Federation in Boca Raton, Florida. In addition to his work in fundraising, Ted was also director of the Jewish Community Relations Council and responsible for the Federation's Jewish education efforts in South Palm Beach County. With a lifelong commitment to the Jewish community, Ted received his bachelor's degree in psychology at Roosevelt University in Chicago and a Masters of Arts and ordination form the Jewish Theological Seminary in New York. After fourteen years in congregational work, Ted entered the community agency system. Ted has two adult children, Aviva and Josh, living in Florida and New York.

Gordon M. Freeman has served as rabbi of Congregation B'nai Shalom in Walnut Creek, California, since 1968. He has been a post-doctoral fellow and scholar-in-residence in the Political Science Department, University of California, Berkeley. His research and writing has been concerned with the Jewish political tradition. In addition, he is co-editor of *Morh Derekh*, the rabbi's manual published by the Rabbinical Assembly.

Rabbi Freeman is a Hebrew calligrapher. He and his wife Susan have four daughters and four grandchildren.

Stuart Kelman is the founding rabbi of Congregation Netivot Shalom in Berkeley, California. His ordination is from the Jewish Theological Seminary of America, and he holds a PhD from the University of Southern California in the field of education. Previously, he was the executive director of the Agency for Jewish Education of the Greater East Bay and was Assistant Professor of Education at Hebrew Union College in Los Angeles. He has worked extensively in Jewish education, editing *What We Know About Jewish Education*; serving as one of the founding members of the Coalition for the Advancement of Jewish Education (CAJE). He has written extensively about bikkur cholim (visiting the sick), death and dying, and gays and lesbians in a Conservative synagogue. He is married to Vicky Kelman, a Jewish family educator, and they have four children and one grandchild.

Rose Levinson is the founding director of the *Tiferet* Project. Her essays on contemporary Jewish issues, such as the role of women and the significance of the synagogue in urban life, have appeared in a number of publications. In addition, she teaches college literature, with a speciality in nineteenth century British and Russian fiction. Rose is also the host of a weekly radio program on public policy issues. She and her partner David are blessed with Tamsin and Alex, their London-based family, and Matt, Amy and Sara in Chicago.

Rabbi Harry A. Manhoff has a PhD in Comparative Religions, specializing in Christian origins, from the University of California, Santa Barbara. He received his AB from Yale in Philosophy of Religion. After ordination, he received a presidential fellowship for post-graduate studies at Columbia University in Ancient Semitics. Recently Rabbi Manhoff was awarded a DD from the Hebrew Union College - Jewish Institute of Religion celebrating his twenty-five years in the rabbinate. Married to Barbara for over thirty years, he is the father of three children, Rinat, Shai and Eitan. Besides serving Temple Beth Sholom in San Leandro, California; Rabbi Manhoff is a lecturer at St. Mary's College in Moraga and California State University, Hayward. When not teaching, preaching or writing, Rabbi Manhoff is an avid baseball and football fan, and collector of graphic novels.

Glenn Massarano is a lay leader at Congregation Netivot Shalom in Berkeley, California, where he participates on the ritual committee, functions as kashrut (kosher) coordinator, and is a teacher of Torah reading and other liturgical skills. His "day job" is as a systems engineer, building traffic management systems. He lives in Berkeley, California, along with his wife, Judy, and two sons Sa'adia and Betzalel.

Rabbi Mimi Weisel is currently rabbi-in-residence at the Jewish Community High School of the Bay in San Francisco where she is responsible for the Jewish academic and spiritual life of the school. She is also an adjunct member of the faculty at the Ziegler School of Rabbinic Studies at the University of Judaism in Los Angeles, where she previously served as assistant dean. Rabbi Weisel has experience teaching Jewish adult education in a wide variety of settings, including community courses in Los Angeles and Miami, and seminars on spirituality for Jewish educators. She was ordained at the Jewish Theological Seminary in 1998. Prior to becoming a rabbi, she spent a dozen years in human resources management in a large aerospace firm. Her husband, Paul Hamburg, is librarian for the Judaica collection at UC Berkeley.